# AI Foundations of Large Language Models

Jon Adams

# CONTENTS

# INTRODUCTION

Welcome to 'AI Foundations of Large Language Models', your gateway to understanding the computational marvels shaping our digital era. This book marks the beginning of your journey into the realm of Large Language Models—those intricate algorithms capable of crafting text so human, it might just make you do a double-take.

Envisioned for both the curious novice and the tech enthusiast, this volume lays the groundwork, unveiling the fascinating chronicle of LLMs from their inception to their role as powerhouses in modern AI research and application. The pages within will navigate you through the evolution of LLMs, unraveling how simple strings of code matured into entities capable of composing poetry, coding software, and chatting like old friends.

With a commitment to clarity, we break down the complex gears of LLM operations, demystifying the mechanics behind how they parse human language and generate their own convincing narratives. Yet, this is no dry textbook; it's a vibrant tale of innovation and ingenuity. Imagine peering over the shoulders of the greatest minds in AI as they lay the keystones of what would become the foundation of cognitive computing.

By the end of this volume, you will have gained not just an introductory understanding of LLMs but an appreciation for their profound implications on society. 'AI Foundations of Large Language Models' promises to equip you with the knowledge to not only grasp how these technologies work but also to fathom their potential to revolutionize our interaction with machines—and with each other. Welcome aboard this exploration of digital intelligence; where it leads is limited only by the farthest reaches of our collective imagination.

# THE EMERGENCE OF LANGUAGE MODELS

An exploration of the key milestones in the development of language models, from early computational linguistics to the advent of transformer-based architectures.

Imagine stepping into a world where the words you speak or type could be understood by machines as easily as by your closest friends. This is the domain of language models—smart programs designed to grasp and use human language in a way that was once the realm of science fiction. Our journey through the history of these models is much like following a river from its source to the sea; it begins humbly, with small streams of innovation that grow and join, eventually leading to a vast and powerful current of capabilities. We'll walk through each step, from the first attempts to teach computers basic grammar, to the intricate systems that now predict and generate text, giving you a clear view of how each part contributes to the whole. Think of it as learning the secret recipe of how words stir these programs to life. By the end, you'll see how these developments aren't just for tech experts—they shape the way we all communicate, shop, and even have fun with our gadgets. Let's explore this fascinating evolution together, making sense of the technical wizardry in a way that's as clear and straightforward as having a chat over coffee.

A language model is like a digital brain that's been taught the patterns of human speech. It's a type of software that has absorbed a huge amount of text—books, articles, conversations—and learned how to predict what word comes next in a sentence, like a well-read friend guessing the end of your sentence. Think about the times you've started typing an email and your phone suggests your next word; that's a language model at work. But it's not just about playing a guessing game with words; these models are crafted to understand context. For example, they know that "bank" can mean the side of a river as well as a place to keep money, depending on the rest of your sentence. The magic of these models lies in their ability to weave words together in ways that make sense and, at times, even creatively express ideas, allowing computers to respond to your typing or verbal questions in a way that feels almost human. In a world where we're constantly interacting online, language models stand behind the scenes, powering everything from search engines giving us just the right results, to chatbots that help us with customer service, making our digital lives smoother and more intuitive.

Let's look at the way language models learn to grasp and process our language. To start, imagine a language model as a student, where the world's text is their textbook. They begin by reading, or rather, processing vast heaps of text data – from blogs and books to everyday dialogues. This data collection is their first step in training; it's where they observe how words and sentences flow in multiple contexts.

Before this student can learn from all this data, it has to be organized, which is part of a step called preprocessing. Here, the text is cleaned up – basically stripping out anything that doesn't help in understanding language structures, like unwanted characters or formatting. It's akin to underlining the important parts in a textbook, making everything easier to study.

Next comes the core of the learning phase. This involves a specific type of artificial intelligence called a neural network, which functions a bit like the brain's network of neurons. A language model has multiple layers in this network, each specializing in a different part of language comprehension. One layer might focus on recognizing the grammar, another on understanding the sentiment, and yet another might work to differentiate between the various meanings of a word like 'bank'.

These layers work in concert to predict what comes next in a sentence by assigning probabilities to each possible word. As it trains, the language model sharpens its predictions through repetition and correction, learning from mistakes, similar to practice tests before the final exam. This part of the process involves pattern recognition – where the model identifies patterns in the way words are used – and refinement, where it continually improves itself.

When it comes to understanding a word with multiple meanings, it's all about context. The model uses its trained patterns to consider the words around 'bank' to figure out whether it's land beside a river or a place to keep money. It looks for clues in the surrounding words and their usual associations to make an educated guess.

Digging deeper, algorithmic decision-making refers to how the model uses its layers to arrive at these educated guesses. These aren't random; they're the product of a complex but well-ordered system assessing probabilities – a never-ending cycle of prediction, feedback, and adjustment.

The elegance of these models lies in their blend of simplicity and depth. Though they capture complex patterns in language, the core idea is basic: read, recognize patterns, and use these patterns to make smart guesses. And by doing this over and over, language models become adept at understanding and generating human language, shaping the way we interact with technology, making our digital experiences feel almost seamlessly human.

Picture the earliest language models as the most basic flip phones, capable of rudimentary text communication, but without the finesse or depth of a modern smartphone. In those early days, the task was simple: recognize and follow preset rules, much like the early cell phones that could only send simple text messages scripted beforehand.

As technology advanced, so did language models. They transformed from flip phones to feature phones with added functionalities like quick-reply texts—still limited, but starting to adapt to a user's common phrases. This was the era of statistical models which, unlike their rule-based ancestors, began to detect patterns in language, predicting which word might come next based on frequency, much like a feature phone's predictive text beginning to learn from your typing habits.

Then came the smartphone revolution in language models – neural networks. These are akin to today's intelligent predictive text on steroids. Imagine typing a message on your phone and it not only suggests the next word but forms complete, sensible responses, often predicting what you want to say before you finish typing. Neural networks made this possible by multitudes of 'mini-predictors'—neurons—working parallel to analyze the context and craft coherent pieces of text.

Layer upon layer, these networks stack like the applications on a smartphone, each providing a unique service, from spelling corrections to voice commands. They become more intricate, building texts that are not only coherently structured but contextually appropriate—not unlike a conversational AI that can book your appointments or draft emails that sound eerily like you.

And finally, we reach the present—the cusp of the LLM era, where language models are not just smart but astonishingly intuitive, learning not from scripts and set phrases but from reading almost all the text available on the web, understanding nuances, emotions, and contexts, much like a friend who knows you so well, they finish your sentences and recommend your next favorite book.

In this world of texts, tweets, and terabytes, language models have evolved from basic rule-following machines to sophisticated partners in dialogue, learning from the endless sea of human communication to better serve our needs, guide our searches, and seamlessly weave into the fabric of our daily digital lives.

Here is the breakdown on how neural networks drive language models, making them smart enough to understand and produce human language:

## Neural Networks and Deep Learning for Language Models

- **Input Layer**: The first point of contact where raw text data is fed into the model.

- Processes words or characters as numerical values that the model can understand.

- Often uses techniques like one-hot encoding to convert text into a binary form.

- **Hidden Layers**: Made up of multiple levels of neurons that recognize patterns and intricacies in the data.

- Each neuron weighs the input it receives, applies a function, and passes on the result.

- Some layers may focus on simple structures like common phrases or grammar rules (syntax).

- Other, deeper layers might work on understanding the meaning behind sentences (semantics) or the intended use of language depending on context (pragmatics).

- **Output Layer**: The endpoint that yields the final prediction, such as the next word likely to follow a given sentence.

- This could be a single word, a tag indicating a type of speech, or a probability distribution over many potential outputs.

## Training Neural Networks: The Learning Process

- **Data Collection**: Gathering a vast assortment of text data from different sources for training.

- **Preprocessing**: Cleaning and organizing the data for efficient learning.

- **Backpropagation**: Adjusting the weights of the connections in the network based on errors in prediction, helping the model learn over time.

- Involves forward passing where data moves through the layers to make a prediction and backward passing for error correction.

- **Optimization**: Techniques like gradient descent are used to find the best set of weights and functions to minimize prediction errors.

- Role of Data In Shaping Neural Networks

- **Volume of Data**: The larger the dataset, the more robust and nuanced the language model's understanding.

- **Quality of Data**: Clean, diverse, and context-rich data leads to a more accurate and sophisticated language model.

- **Examples and Variations**: Including different contexts, slang, and language styles to ensure the model learns the variety in human language use.

- Context Interpretation and Meaning Disambiguation

- **Embeddings**: Vectors that help models grasp semantic meaning based on context by placing similar meaning words closer together in multi-dimensional space.

- Allows the model to understand 'bank' as financial institute or riverside based on nearby words.

- **Attention Mechanisms**: Helps the model to focus on relevant parts of the input when making predictions.

- Acts like a highlighter, emphasizing important information that influences the understanding of a word or sentence.

By understanding each component's role in this intricate system, one sees how neural networks contribute to creating language models that can converse, write, and understand human language remarkably well. It's like piecing together a complex puzzle, where every piece is data and each group of pieces forms layers that, altogether, create a full picture of human communication. This model doesn't just repeat patterns; it learns to understand the context and nuances, achieving the complexity necessary for grasping the full spectrum of our language.

In the beginning, language models were like librarians who could only recommend books if you asked for them by using the exact library index code. They were based on strict rules; hard-coded scripts that told a computer how to understand and produce language in very specific cases. But language is vast and unpredictable, filled with quirks, idioms, and expressions that don't follow rigid patterns. To capture this fluidity, the field turned towards statistical approaches, akin to that same librarian now able to recommend new books based on what others are reading or saying about them.

Key to this shift was an understanding that language isn't just a list of rules—it's a living, breathing form of expression that constantly evolves. Statistical models thrive on this reality. They learn by examining large volumes of text, identifying the likelihood of certain words following others, leading to predictions that sound more natural—think of a smartphone autocorrecting text, often with remarkable accuracy. For artificial intelligence, this transition meant a leap from stilted, robotic responses to smooth, almost conversational interactions. Suddenly, the field opened up; where once there was only a narrow path dictated by pre-set instructions, there now lay a whole landscape to explore, map, and understand through patterns and probabilities, giving creators of AI systems the tools to craft solutions that genuinely understand and respond to human nuance. This change didn't just refine AI—it transformed the relationship between machines and human language, taking it closer to how it's naturally used in everyday life.

In the world of language processing, statistical models start their journey with the collection of data, a step we can think of as their school phase where they learn from the sheer variety of language used in real life. This data comes from books, articles, social media, and anywhere language is used. Before the model can learn from it, the text has to be preprocessed. This means breaking it down into manageable pieces called tokens – a process known as tokenization. It's like chopping vegetables before cooking; it's organized and ready to be used. Normalization is the next step where all the text is standardized – for example, 'Email' and 'email' would be treated as the same word, despite the capital E.

After the data is ready, algorithms come into play. One of the workhorses of statistical models is the n-gram algorithm. An n-gram is simply a sequence of 'n' words taken from the text. Predictions are made based on how frequently certain sequences appear. So, if 'apple pie' is a common pairing in the data, the model will predict 'pie' as a likely follow-up to 'apple' in a sentence.

Here's a simple example. For the context of 'apple', the model scours through all the text it's seen and remembers where 'apple' appears. If 'apple' often appears with words like 'eat' or 'fruit', it'll lean towards the fruit meaning. But if it's surrounded by words like 'technology' or 'iPhone', the model will know we're talking about the tech giant.

Now, it's one thing to talk about it, but let's look at what pseudo code for a simple n-gram model calculating the probability of the next word could look like:

```
function getNextWordProbabilities(currentWords):

    counts = {}

    for each n-gram in trainingData:

        if n-gram starts with currentWords:

            nextWord = n-gram following currentWords

            if nextWord in counts:

                counts[nextWord] += 1

            else:

                counts[nextWord] = 1

    totalOccurrences = sum(counts.values())

    probabilities = {word: (count/totalOccurrences) for word, count in counts.items()}

    return probabilities
```

This pseudo code is a blueprint, an outline that describes how we could program a language model to look at data (collected phrases) and count how often each word follows currentWords. By dividing these counts, we find out the likelihood, or 'probability', of what the next word could be. This simple ratio – how many times a word appears versus all the possible options – makes up the very fundamentals of statistical language modeling.

Let's remember that all this isn't just academic – it powers the predictive text on your phone, the voice recognition in virtual assistants, and so much more. Understanding the steps— collection, preprocessing, algorithm application—is like piecing together a puzzle that reveals how technology can understand and even predict our language.

Imagine a bustling city inside your head, where each building represents a neuron, and the roads connecting them are like synapses in the brain. Neural networks in AI are remarkably similar to this intricate urban layout. Like city pathways bustling with messages, each 'neuron' in a neural network receives signals – bits of language data – and then, based on those messages, decides where to send its own signal next.

In processing language, these networks function like a team of linguists passing notes to each other, each one scribbling down observations before slipping the note to the next person. Some are experts in grammar, others in the meaning of words, and so on. They work through layers – like a multi-story library with different genres of language on each floor. The first 'neuron' might recognize a letter, the next forms that into a word, and further up they string together sentences. In the highest offices, they analyze the sentiment – is it a complaint, a compliment?

By the time the note reaches the top floor, the neural network has synthesized raw data into meaningful language, ready for a computer to understand and respond almost as naturally as a person would. This system isn't just about stringing words; it's about capturing the essence of human communication – the tones, the pauses, the rhythm. And though these AI networks may not sleep or daydream, they share our capacity to learn and improve, reshaping how we interact with the technological world around us, one word at a time.

In the story of technology's march forward, certain names stand out like beacons, and Alan Turing's is one of the brightest. Turing was a visionary who laid the very foundations for what we now call artificial intelligence. With his conception of the Turing Test, he proposed a world where machines could mimic human conversation so convincingly that we couldn't tell the difference between a person and a program — a concept that whispers through every modern chatbot and digital assistant.

Fast forward to today, and institutions like Google have taken Turing's torch and run with it, pushing language models to breathtaking heights. Google's search engines and voice-activated helpers sift through the vast expanse of the internet to find exactly what we're looking for, often before we're even sure ourselves. They understand our questions, interpret our requests, and even anticipate our needs using algorithms that would seem like magic to those early pioneers.

From Turing's theoretical beginnings to Google's practical applications, these developments share a thread — a relentless pursuit to break down the barriers between human and machine communication. It's a quest that has turned computers from tools that simply compute to companions that can converse. Such progress underscores not only the remarkable ingenuity ingrained in their work but also illuminates the path we're on, towards a future where digital conversations are as rich and natural as any we have face to face.

Let's look at the intricate journey language models have traveled, from the seed of an idea planted by Alan Turing to the complex algorithms that power devices in our hands and homes. Turing introduced the possibility of machines being able to simulate human conversation—a test we now refer to as the Turing Test. This test opened doors to the idea that computers could be more than just calculators; they could potentially interact with us using our own language.

The road from there to here is paved with countless innovations. Machine learning took Turing's concepts and ran full sprint, particularly with the development of neural networks, which mimic the way neurons in the brain interact. These networks create webs of artificial 'neurons' that light up and communicate with each other to process information and learn over time.

In the beginning, algorithms were simple. They could learn patterns in data, but their understanding of language was primitive. Imagine teaching a child to read by pointing at flashcards—early machines learned much in the same way. But today's language models, like those that underlie Google's suite of tools, are more like well-read scholars, flourishing in an expanse of written text.

These models parse human speech—breaking it down into intelligible chunks—analyze the minutiae, and apply context. They consider what words mean together, not just alone, and they adapt when context shifts. For example, when we ask a voice-activated device where the nearest 'bank' is, it needs to discern whether we're looking for a riverbank or a financial institution based on our previous interactions or the words surrounding our request.

The heart of this deep understanding lies in probabilistic models: statistical methods that calculate the likelihood of one word following another or one meaning being more suitable than another in a given scenario. These evolving models become adept at predicting not only what we might ask next but also what answers we're looking for.

Advanced as they are, these algorithms don't just work straight out of the box. They need to be trained, often with massive sets of text data, so they learn the natural ebb and flow of languages. This process is like a meticulous craftsman, honing their skills through practice to create increasingly sophisticated art—the art, in this case, being natural and helpful human-machine conversation.

As we stand on the cusp of new AI horizons, understanding the mechanics of these achievements is not just about grasping the 'how' but also appreciating the 'why'—why it matters that a machine can talk to us, help us, and maybe even understand us. This progression is a testament to human ingenuity, reflecting our enduring pursuit to enhance life with technology, crafting machines that can exist alongside us, not just as tools but as participants in dialogue.

Imagine researchers as a group of intrepid explorers, each setting sail to the unknown seas of artificial intelligence. They set out under a sky brimming with questions rather than stars, navigating not by constellations but by the faint glow of curiosity. Their quest to create machines that can understand and generate human language has always been as daunting as a vast ocean that's as promising as it is perilous.

Each new discovery brought with it a set of formidable challenges, like puzzling mazes in uncharted islands. At first, the simple act of teaching computers the basics of language seemed like a daunting cliff too sheer to scale. The early rule-based systems were rigid and cumbersome, akin to overly cautious maps that lacked the detail of the rough terrain ahead.

But these explorers of knowledge persisted, making breakthroughs that replaced rigidity with flexibility, much like discovering a new compass that points towards possibilities beyond the horizon. The arrival of neural networks was a momentous occasion, like a burst of wind filling the sails, pushing the boundaries of what was achievable. They began charting courses through the use of statistical models, uncovering patterns in language akin to recognizing currents and using them to navigate.

Each hurdle crossed led to smarter, more capable language models – from crude signposts to sophisticated guides conversing with travelers in their native tongue. Researchers learned to harness vast amounts of data, a windfall of riches that fed into learning algorithms, making AI systems more adept, more eloquent, and vastly more intuitive.

Just like any good story of adventure, the journey of AI research isn't without its tales of mishaps and wrong turns. But each one was an opportunity to learn, adapt, and refine, forging a path through uncharted wakes towards a future where human and machine can share a language and maybe, one day, stories of their own adventures side by side.

Here is the breakdown on the evolution of language models:

**Rule-Based Systems:**

- **Early Systems**: Language understanding was based on a fixed set of rules created by programmers.

- Example: If the system saw the word "weather," it had rules to provide a weather report.

- **Limitations**: These systems lacked flexibility and couldn't handle the vast variety of human language.

- Shift to Statistical Language Models:

- **Introduction of Statistics**: The realization that language is too complex for rigid rules led to statistical approaches.

- Example: Text was analyzed for word frequencies and patterns to predict next words.

- **Probabilistic Models**: Systems now used probability calculations to make decisions.

- Sublist: Bayes' Theorem and Markov Models were employed to improve predictions based on prior occurrences.

- Advent of Machine Learning:

- **Learning from Data**: Rather than relying on hand-coded rules, models began to learn directly from linguistic data.

- Systems used large text corpora to 'learn' language.

- **Pattern Recognition**: Algorithms detected recurring patterns to improve understanding and response generation.

- Neural networks allowed systems to recognize complex patterns.

- Deep Learning and Neural Networks:

- **Deep Neural Networks**: Models with multiple layers that could learn subtleties of language representation.

- Each layer of the network learns different features of language.

- **Recurrent Neural Networks (RNNs)**: Specialized in processing sequences, like sentences.

- Captured information from previous words to inform the understanding of current and future words.

- **Long Short-Term Memory Networks (LSTMs)**: An advancement of RNNs that was better at retaining long-term context.

- Contemporary Advances:

- **Attention Mechanisms**: Allowed models to focus on relevant parts of the input data.

- Example: Focuses on 'crust' when predicting the next word after 'apple' in a discussion about pie.

- **Transformers**: Introduced structures that better capture contextual information without reliance on sequential data processing.

- Enabled huge leaps in language generation quality with models like GPT and BERT.

- Integration into Applications:

- **Practical Use Cases**: These advanced language models are now found in voice-activated GPS, digital assistants, and more.

- They continuously learn from new data to offer more fluid, intuitive interactions.

- **Data Feedback Loops**: Contemporary AI not only uses language but also learns from the interaction, allowing continuous improvement.

This granular look at each component's development showcases the remarkable path from the dream of intelligent machines to today's reality where AI can communicate effectively, carrying on Turing's legacy and paving the way for even smarter future technologies.

The story of Large Language Models (LLMs) begins not with a bang, but with a blueprint—the theoretical structures that laid the groundwork for what would become a transformative force in AI. The journey from basic programming to the sophisticated entities that are LLMs today is akin to laying a complex web of roads across an entire country. Initially, there were simple, direct routes—algorithmic paths that could carry only certain types of language data, like early voice recognition systems that required exact phrases to operate. But as innovations piled up, the roads became highways, and the highways interlinked into vast networks able to carry a much denser flow of information.

These colossal systems were built on the bedrock of statistical learning, where machines, thirsty for knowledge, drank in the linguistic patterns from a sea of text data. By deciphering these patterns, AI began to anticipate language with impressive accuracy. LLMs, the latest travelers on these highways, didn't just navigate existing roads—they constructed new pathways, making connections far beyond what was once thought possible.

Today's LLMs have turned what began as a slow transfer of information into high-speed processing and generation of human-like text. They've scaled mountains of data to understand context and nuances, leading to AI capabilities that excel in translating languages, powering customer service bots, and creating content that feels incredibly authentic. The impact is undeniable: LLMs have shifted the very foundation of technology's role in society, taking us from rigidly structured interactions to a fluid dance of human-computer communication that continues to evolve and astonish.

Let's look at the intricate evolution of Large Language Models (LLMs). Beginning with the early days of language understanding, we saw algorithms that could be equated to simple tools—useful but very basic. These early models had their roots in rule-based systems that functioned by following explicit programming instructions, but they struggled to grapple with the complexity and variability of human language.

As the limitations of these systems became apparent, the emergence of statistical models marked a significant turning point. These models didn't rely on hard-coded rules; instead, they learned from examples. Imagine a chef tasting different regional dishes to understand local cuisines rather than following a single recipe book. Researchers started to compile extensive datasets—massive collections of text from books, articles, and the web—to feed into these models.

Processing such large datasets required meticulous preparation, much like a librarian cataloging books for a library. This data needed to be cleaned, organized, and converted into a format suitable for machine learning—a process known as preprocessing. And just as the penchant for learning from others' experiences can enrich understanding, transfer learning allowed LLMs to build upon previous models' knowledge, jumping ahead in the learning process rather than starting from scratch.

A game-changer in LLMs' development was the introduction of attention mechanisms—tools that let models focus on specific parts of the text, similar to how a spotlight on a stage directs an audience's focus. With this, LLMs could sift through irrelevant information and pay closer attention to contextual cues, enhancing their comprehension and ability to interact in more nuanced ways.

All these technological advancements paved the way for LLMs to undertake complex tasks like translating languages with nuances that resonate with human sensibilities or creating content that adapts to various styles and form. Behind their seemingly magical capabilities lies a sophisticated architecture of neural networks—multiple layers that each learn different aspects of language, from the structure of sentences to the subtleties of meaning.

These models are not static; they are constantly learning and evolving. Through multiple iterations and refinements, they've become adept at not only understanding the written word but also generating it in ways that can seem startlingly human. This progress has smashed barriers in AI, allowing for interactions between humans and machines that were once confined to the realms of imagination.

As we close this chapter, let's look back at the path we've traveled to understand language models and their monumental role in today's AI. We started with the simplest form of language models, rule-based systems that were as rigid as set tracks on a railroad—limited in direction and flexibility. We then moved onto the advent of statistical models, which were like gardeners tending to plants, nurturing the data and observing patterns to produce more natural text predictions.

From there, we witnessed the rise of neural networks, a significant leap that transformed our garden into a lush, interconnected forest of possibilities. These advanced models mimicked the way our brains work, using layers upon layers to contextualize and generate language. The culmination of this journey is found in the Large Language Models that drive many of the AI applications we use every day—from virtual assistants on our phones to translation services that break down language barriers.

It's a story of continuous progress, where each milestone was not just a step forward but an opening of new opportunities. It has made the once distant dream of AI that can truly understand and interact with us an everyday reality. The implications are profound, reshaping everything from how we gather information to how we connect with each other across the globe. And yet, this journey is far from over. With each new development, we edge closer to a world where the line between human and machine communication becomes ever more seamless.

# FOUNDATIONS OF NEURAL NETWORKS

Welcome to the entrancing realm of neural networks, the hidden architects of artificial intelligence that we interact with every single day. Much like the intricate wiring in a complex machine, these networks form the inner workings of systems that can recognize faces, suggest the music we might enjoy, and even drive cars. At their core, neural networks are inspired by our own brains, composed of interconnected units that learn from experience to make decisions. This introductory journey will unravel how such networks come to life, process vast streams of data, and evolve into being so astoundingly good at tasks that were formerly the exclusive domain of humans. Step by step, we'll walk through their structure, how they're trained and fine-tuned, ultimately shaping the AI that both subtly and significantly impacts our daily lives. So, let's begin this exploration with a sense of wonder, ready to demystify these technologies with a clear and friendly guide that turns the complex into the comprehensible.

Neural networks are a series of algorithms, kind of like a sequence of steps, that aim to recognize underlying relationships in a set of data through a process that mimics the way the human brain operates. At their heart, they are made up of 'neurons', which you can think of as tiny processing units that work together to solve complex problems. Each neuron takes in input, like numbers or data points, does a bit of computation, and then passes on its results. As information moves through layers of these neurons, the network can learn to make sense of the input—identifying patterns or making decisions.

For example, when you show a neural network a collection of photos, it might learn to tell which ones include trees by recognizing the pattern of a trunk and branches, even if no one tells it what a tree looks like. This is the network training itself by analyzing examples, much like learning by practice instead of by rules. It's this ability to learn from data and get better over time that makes neural networks a cornerstone for modern AI— they help your phone recognize your voice, online services translate languages, and can even aid doctors in diagnosing diseases from medical images.

Simple though it may sound, a neural network's knack for pattern recognition is how it turns raw data into actionable insight, serving as the engine behind the AI that's becoming more intertwined with everyday life. And as you might join a gym to get fit, neural networks can be 'trained' to get better at their tasks, continuously improving, adapting, and making even smarter decisions as they 'learn.'

Neural networks come in various forms, each designed for specific kinds of tasks. To grasp their architecture, think of them like unique blueprints for buildings, each layout tailored for different purposes.

A simple feedforward neural network, for example, consists of an input layer, hidden layers, and an output layer. Information travels in one direction: from input to output. Below is a simplified pseudo code outline illustrating how a feedforward neural network processes input and updates its weights—a process known as backpropagation:

```
function feedforward(inputs, weights) {

  let activations = inputs;
  for each layer in weights {

    activations = applyActivation(dotProduct(weights[layer], activations));

  }
  return activations;

}
function backpropagate(error, weights, learning_rate) {

  for each layer in weights reversed {

    let layer_error = dotProduct(error, transpose(weights[layer]));

    let gradient = multiply(error, derivativeActivation(weights[layer]));

    weights[layer] = updateWeights(weights[layer], gradient, learning_rate);

    error = layer_error;

  }

}
```

The 'applyActivation' function represents the activation function, which is a mathematical equation that determines whether a neuron will be activated or not—think of it as a filter deciding if the information is relevant. These functions add non-linearity to the network, allowing it to learn complex data patterns. Common examples include the sigmoid, tanh, and ReLU functions.

The cost function measures how well the network performs. Imagine a sharpshooter practicing at a target range—the closer the marks to the bullseye, the better the performance. In neural network training, this 'bullseye' is the minimal error, and the cost function guides the training towards it.

Lastly, the term 'gradient' refers to the use of gradients in updating the network. Think of it as a compass for the network, pointing the direction to adjust the weights to improve predictions. This use of gradients—known as gradient descent—is akin to finding the fastest way downhill.

Through repeated cycles of processing input, evaluating error, and adjusting weights, the neural network becomes more accurate, thereby 'learning' from its experiences, much like an apprentice improving a craft with each attempt. This meticulous process is the essence of how neural networks evolve over time, laying down the foundation for sophisticated tasks they perform, from voice recognition to predictive texting.

Picture a neural network as a multi-story building where data enters at the ground floor and visits every level to be transformed into meaningful information. The ground floor is the input layer, where the network first receives the raw data, be it images, sound, or text. This data isn't much use on its own – much like raw ingredients in a kitchen before they are cooked into a meal.

As data moves up to the next floors, or the hidden layers, the transformation begins. Each of these floors specializes in different tasks. One might identify edges in an image, another might recognize shapes, and so on, akin to different chefs in a restaurant kitchen, each preparing a component of the final dish. Each neuron, or 'chef,' in these layers does its own simple calculation before passing the results on to the next layer. The neurons work simultaneously, processing inputs and their connections – the synapses – adjust or 'learn,' based on the accuracy of their output.

By the time the data reaches the penthouse, or the output layer, it has been processed through all these layers and has taken on a new, refined form – a decision or a prediction. Here, the network uses everything it has learned to make a final judgment, like a head chef tasting a dish before it is served, ensuring it meets the standard.

The flow is seamless, with each layer's output becoming the next layer's input, learning and adapting every time new data comes through the front door. This process is what allows neural networks to make decisions, recognize speech, translate languages, and so much more, growing more intelligent and efficient with every piece of data they process. It's an exquisite machine of learning, turning the unknown into the understood, a testament to the power of layered collaboration.

Let's look at the inner activities that happen in a neural network's hidden layers. These layers are where the real 'thinking' gets done, as they process the initial data received by the network. Each neuron in these layers performs a calculation that might seem simple on its own but is part of a complex web of operations.

A neuron's calculation involves weights and biases. You can think of weights as the importance given to incoming data — certain features might be weighted more heavily if they are better indicators for making predictions. Biases act like fine-tuning dials, allowing the neural network to better fit the data, even when all inputs are zero.

When a neuron receives data, it multiplies the data by its weights and adds the bias. However, this is still a linear equation, and real-world data is anything but linear. This is where activation functions come in. They introduce non-linearity, allowing neurons to make sense of more complex patterns. Common examples are ReLU (Rectified Linear Unit) and sigmoid functions — the ReLU provides a simple 'if positive, pass through; if negative, output zero,' while the sigmoid squashes values into a range between 0 and 1, useful for binary decisions.

Once the network generates an output, backpropagation begins. This is where the network learns from any mistakes it made. It starts by calculating the error, which is the difference between the predicted output and the actual output. The network then goes backward, from the output layer to the input layer, adjusting weights and biases to decrease the error — a bit like a golfer analyzing swings to avoid sand traps and improve future shots.

During backpropagation, each weight's adjustment is based on its contribution to the error and is scaled by the learning rate — how quickly the model learns. Too fast and it may overshoot the best solution, too slow and it might never get there. This intricate adjustment process, carried out across all neurons, is what helps a neural network fine-tune its decision-making, leading to improved accuracy over time.

This comprehensive machinery — input, weight and bias computation with activation, and learning from errors through backpropagation — encapsulates the astonishing capability of neural networks to learn from data, make decisions, and ultimately power the AI systems in our lives. It's a delicate balance of mathematics and programming, honed to interpret the complexities of our world.

Training a neural network is akin to teaching a child to recognize patterns by using blocks of different shapes and colors. First, you introduce the blocks—this is the data feeding stage. The network looks at examples—say, photos labeled as either 'cat' or 'no cat.' Each photo is broken down into pixels, which serve as the input data, and each pixel has a value. Think of these pixel values as the various attributes of the blocks, such as shape or hue.

Next, the network starts sorting—inside, it's made up of layers, and every layer is responsible for identifying certain features. It might be 'whiskers' in one layer, 'tail' in another. These features are recognized through weights, which are adjustable variables attached to each bit of input data. At first, these weights are set randomly.

Imagine asking the child to sort the blocks without prior knowledge—the first sorting attempt likely won't be perfect. Similarly, the network's initial guesses are usually off. So, the network compares its guesses to the correct answers, computes the difference—or error—for each photo, and then uses this error to adjust the weights in a process called backpropagation. In essence, it's learning from its mistakes.

By adjusting the weights, the network 'learns' which features are important for distinguishing a cat. Over many cycles of guessing, checking, and adjusting—much like a child repeatedly playing with blocks—the network gets better at making accurate predictions.

Finally, the performance improvement is constantly measured, ensuring that for every batch of photos, the network is, indeed, getting better at "seeing" cats, just as a child would get better at identifying and sorting blocks into the right groups. Over time, this process enables the neural network to understand and identify patterns with a high degree of accuracy, evolving into a powerful tool capable of performing complex recognition tasks.

Here is the breakdown on how neural networks process data and learn to make predictions:

**Feature Detection:**

   - **Input Layer**: Receives raw data (like pixels in an image).

   - **Convolutional Layers**:

      - Use filters to scan the input for features (such as edges and textures).

      - Preserve the spatial relationship between pixels to identify patterns.   ´

      - Output is a feature map indicating the presence of certain features in the input.

   - Reducing Dimensionality:

   - **Pooling Layers**:

      - Follow convolutional layers to reduce the size of the feature map.

- Makes the output less sensitive to the exact location of features in the input.

- Typically, max pooling is used to take the largest value in a window of the feature map.

- Classification or Regression:

- **Fully Connected Layers**:

- All neurons in these layers have connections to all activations from the previous layer.

- Combine features to make final predictions.

- Output layer typically uses a softmax function for classification to represent probabilities or a linear function for regression problems.

- Learning from Errors – Backpropagation:

- **Calculating Error**:

- The difference between the predicted output and the actual output is quantified using a loss function.

- **Backpropagation**:

- Propagates the error back through the network, from the output layer to the input layer.

- Adjusts the weights and biases of neurons based on their contribution to the error.

- Weight Adjustment via Gradient Descent:

- **Gradients**:

- Measures how much a change in weights will change the error.

- **Learning Rate**:

- Determines how big a step to take in the direction opposite to the gradient (also known as gradient descent).

- A high learning rate could overshoot the lowest error, while a low rate might take too long or get stuck in local minima.

- Iterative Optimization:

- The network repeats this process over many iterations (epochs), each time improving the accuracy of predictions by fine-tuning weights and biases.

- Continuously monitored and tested to ensure improvement in performance.

By repeating these steps, the neural network essentially teaches itself how to make better decisions based on the data it receives. It's a meticulous and fascinating process where simple mathematical adjustments translate into a network capable of performing tasks with increasing competence.

Imagine a neural network as a person faced with the challenge of learning a new language. At first, everything sounds foreign, just as raw data appears as a meaningless array of numbers to the network. The initial step is like learning the alphabet or common phrases—simple and repetitive. Just as a language learner begins to recognize the patterns of sounds and grammar that form words and sentences, a neural network identifies patterns within the data.

The learning process involves listening to the language used in context, practicing with a few words, then sentences, and eventually having full conversations. Through trial and error, and with plenty of practice, the language learner starts to understand more and can even predict what might be said next in a conversation.

Similarly, as raw data flows through the neural network's layers, each layer takes on the role of learning a more complex aspect of the 'language' within the data. The first layer might identify simple patterns, such as whether a sound is loud or soft. Subsequent layers might learn to recognize the tone, then the rhythm, and finally understand the meaning and respond appropriately, like piecing together syllables to form words and sentences.

With each new piece of data, the neural network refines its understanding, improving its predictive capabilities—much like a person becoming more fluent in a new language over time. This is how a complex dataset is translated into sophisticated language by a neural network, enabling it to perform tasks such as translating speech or writing poetry. It's not just about decoding; it's about developing an intuitive grasp of the complexities of language through continued learning and adaptation.

Neural networks are like the secret wizards behind the curtain, making the gadgets and services we use every day seem magically in tune with our needs. Take the smartphone in your pocket—it can recognize your face, even if you're wearing a new hat or you've decided to grow a beard. That's a neural network at work, adapting and learning your features so you don't have to type in a passcode every time.

Or consider how streaming services seem to know just the right movie to recommend after a long day. That's not happenstance; it's a neural network sifting through your watch history, learning from what you love and what you leave halfway through. The result? A personalized lineup that feels like it was curated by a close friend.

Online, neural networks are the power behind those helpful chatbots that pop up to assist you. They understand your typed questions and provide real-time responses, mimicking human conversation. It's like having a personal concierge guiding you through website mazes to find just what you're looking for.

The beauty of neural networks lies in their ability to grasp the complex tapestry of human preference, habit, and expression—turning that understanding into responsive, intuitive experiences. These networks don't just follow commands; they anticipate, adapt, and make our daily digital interactions feel almost effortlessly natural. In weaving such seamless integration into the fabric of our lives, neural networks have reshaped what we expect from technology, bringing it closer than ever to a reflection of our human essence.

Here is the breakdown on how neural networks function

within specific technologies:

### Facial Recognition on Smartphones:

#### - Image Preprocessing:

- Adjust lighting and color contrast to normalize varying conditions.

- Detect and align facial features to a standard format.

#### - Feature Detection:

- Locate key features such as eyes, nose, and mouth.

- Analyze the unique aspects like the distance between eyes or the shape of the jawline.

#### - Pattern Classification:

- Match detected features with known patterns stored in the neural network.

- Confirm identity based on the likelihood of a feature set match.

### Streaming Service Recommendations:

- ## Collaborative Filtering:

- Gathers viewing data from many users to find common patterns.

- Recommends content watched by those with similar tastes.

- ## Content-Based Filtering:

- Analyzes the details of the content you have enjoyed, such as genre, actors, or director.

- Suggests new content with similar attributes to what you have liked before.

## Chatbots:

- ## Natural Language Processing (NLP):

- Parse user input to understand the language structure and words used.

- Detect slang or misspellings to maintain communication effectiveness.

- ## Intent Recognition:

- Discern the user's goal or need from their input (e.g., booking a ticket, finding information).

- Categorize input into predefined intentions for appropriate response handling.

- **Response Generation:**

- Select or generate a response that aligns with the recognized intent.

- Adapt phrasing based on previous interactions for more personalized engagement.

In each of these applications, neural networks actively learn and adapt—taking in new data, adjusting their 'understanding,' and refining their outputs. Whether it's enhancing the security and ease of unlocking a phone, personalizing entertainment, or providing efficient customer service, these systems are constantly fine-tuning their responses, making them an indispensable part of our digital experience.

As neural networks grow ever more intricate and capable, the horizon appears dotted with developments that hint at a truly adaptive and personalized future of AI. Imagine neural networks that don't just recognize your face or voice but understand your emotions and respond accordingly, enriching interactions with a layer of empathy previously uncharted in machinery.

Advancements in neural network's abilities to process natural language are on the brink of enabling machines to comprehend and engage in human conversation with the nuance and depth of an attentive companion. This would redefine customer service, education, and even therapy, as AI systems could provide real-time assistance and support, mimicking the understanding of a trusted human advisor.

Future neural networks may also be the craftsmen of creativity, composing music that resonates with our personal tastes or drafting narratives that are indistinguishable from those penned by human authors. They could become our creative collaborators, providing a scaffold upon which our own ideas could intertwine to form truly collaborative works of art.

As these powerful networks become more energy-efficient and less data-hungry, they'll seamlessly integrate into our everyday devices, making technology an even more natural extension of human intention. This shift will likely make today's most cutting-edge technology look quaint by comparison. With each leap forward, neural networks promise to carry us into an era where AI blends invisibly into the fabric of our daily lives, fulfilling the promise of technology as a true enhancer of human capability and experience.

Let's look at the intricate advancements in neural network technology. Delving into sentiment analysis, this involves teaching a neural network to recognize the emotional tone behind human communication. By analyzing text data — words and phrases commonly associated with emotions like joy, anger, or sadness — neural networks learn to detect how someone is feeling. It's like reading between the lines to catch the subtle cues of human emotion, and that could lead to AI that responds not just to what we say but how we say it, adjusting its reactions to fit our emotional state.

When it comes to conversations, neural networks are improving in contextual understanding. They're not just processing individual words, but whole sentences and paragraphs, considering context to grasp the meaning. This shift from keyword spotting to understanding the intent and nuance is significant. It could transform customer service bots from rigid responders into fluid conversationalists capable of genuine interaction, akin to chatting with a friend who remembers past discussions and personal details.

And in creative fields, generative algorithms are at the frontier of neural network technology. These are like the imaginative painters within the AI world, using learned rules to create new content ranging from art to music. These networks sift through massive datasets, identify underlying patterns, and harness these to generate new pieces that are both original and resonate with existing human preferences.

Each of these components — sentiment analysis, contextual understanding, and generative creativity — are piecing together to build a future where AI is not just a tool but a companion and collaborator. The implications of this leap forward extend into every corner of our lives, from stronger human-machine relationships to boundless avenues for creative expression, paving the way for an era where AI becomes a mirror to our intellectual and emotional depths.

Neural networks stand at the heart of AI's evolution, serving as the engine for today's most innovative tools and technologies. These networks mimic the human brain's ability to learn from experience, turning abstract data into actionable insights. They reach into every corner of our lives, from improving medical diagnostics with the precision to pinpoint diseases early, to enhancing the safety of self-driving cars by processing and responding to real-world inputs at lightning speed. Neural networks are also the artisans behind your phone's ability to understand spoken commands and the uncanny knack of social media platforms to suggest content that catches your eye.

Looking ahead, these systems will only grow smarter, more intuitive, and increasingly intertwined with our everyday interactions. They promise to unlock potent solutions to complex problems that once seemed insurmountable, and in doing so, they will recalibrate the way we work, interact, and unleash our creativity. The takeaway is clear: Neural networks don't just represent a technological milestone; they are the catalysts that will continue to redefine human potential, broadening the horizons of what machines can do for—and with—us.

# TRANSFORMERS AND ATTENTION MECHANISMS

You are now in the world of transformers and attention mechanisms, where the marvels of modern AI are unlocking new potential every day. These two groundbreaking innovations are like the engine and the steering wheel of a car: transformers drive the system forward, while attention mechanisms guide it to focus on the right paths. Together, they enable computers to sift through reams of text and not just read the words, but understand the story they're telling.

In this section, you'll learn how transformers can juggle an entire library of information, yet with the finesse of attention mechanisms, pick out just the facts that matter. Without getting tangled in technical jargon, we'll unwrap how this technology is shaping software that can converse intelligently, translate languages with finesse, and even write its own original content.

This intricate dance between transformers and attention is not simply an academic curio; it affects everything from the way we ask for directions to how we interact with our smartphones. By unraveling these AI wonders, you'll gain a deeper appreciation for the silent digital assistants that are rapidly becoming an integral part of our daily lives. So let's step into this fascinating landscape together, exploring and understanding the silent, powerful workings of AI.

Attention mechanisms in AI are a bit like a thoughtful reader who, while going through a page of text, knows to pay more heed to the most meaningful words and phrases. Rather than treating every word with equal merit, these mechanisms assign different weights or importance to each part of the data. It's a way of saying, 'This word here matters a lot for understanding, but that one over there, not so much.'

This system of weighted importance allows AI to manage and interpret vast amounts of text far more effectively. For instance, in a sentence, certain words give context and meaning to others. The attention mechanism can identify and focus on these critical words, enhancing the AI's interpretation of the sentence as a whole. Think of it as a highlighter that marks out the bits that carry the crux of the meaning while leaving the less significant parts in the background.

In practice, when a neural network equipped with an attention mechanism processes a text, it dynamically allocates its 'attention' to different parts of the input data. The result is a more nuanced and accurate understanding of the text, similar to how a human expert reads and interprets a complex document, focusing keenly on the most relevant sections to grasp the overall message. By incorporating attention mechanisms, AI systems gain the ability to sift through the noise and hone in on what truly matters.

In understanding the technical workings of an attention mechanism within a neural network, imagine programming a system to read a book and discern which sentences are most vital to the story's plot. Here is a pseudo code representation, simplified, to explain the computational narrative:

```
function calculate_attention_scores(query, keys, values) {

    let attention_scores = [];

    for (let key of keys) {

        // Calculate the dot product of the query and keys

        let score = dot_product(query, key);

        attention_scores.push(score);

    }
    // Normalize scores using a softmax function

    let attention_weights = softmax(attention_scores);
    // Apply the calculated attention weights to the values

    let weighted_sum = [];

    for (let i = 0; i < values.length; i++) {

        weighted_sum.push(values[i] * attention_weights[i]);

    }
    // Sum the weighted values to produce the final output

    let output = sum(weighted_sum);

    return output;
```

```
}

function softmax(scores) {

    let max_score = Math.max(...scores);

    let exp_scores = scores.map((s) => Math.exp(s - max_score));

    let sum_exp_scores = sum(exp_scores);

    return exp_scores.map((s) => s / sum_exp_scores);

}
```

The `calculate_attention_scores` function illustrates how an attention mechanism determines the relevance of different pieces of data, which in this case are represented by 'keys' and associated 'values'. A 'query' — akin to the current word being processed — interacts with 'keys' to produce attention 'scores', signifying the relevance each key has to the query.

The `softmax` function refines these scores to ensure they are all between 0 and 1, adding up to 1, much like converting a raw score into a percentage. The result is a set of 'attention weights', which denote the amount of attention each piece of data should receive.

Finally, these weights are used to create a 'weighted sum' of 'values', which might represent different elements of the sentence. The summation yields the anticipated output, combining all the relevant pieces of information while diminishing the less relevant ones.

This technique enables the AI to focus — highlight — the

'most telling parts of the page', effectively turning data into a comprehensible output. Authenticate understanding is then just like comprehending the plot of a story by focusing on the key sentences, thanks to the network's learned 'attention'.

Imagine if you will, an attention mechanism in a neural network as a bright neon highlighter in the hands of a meticulous student poring over pages of dense text. With each stroke, the highlighter illuminates key phrases and terms that are crucial for understanding the essence of the material, allowing the student to focus on the most informative parts and piece together the narrative more effectively.

Now, picture this mechanism as a knowledgeable tour guide in a bustling, historic city. Among the maze of streets and landmarks, the guide deftly points out the most significant sites, sharing stories that give depth and color to what might otherwise be an overwhelming array of sights. Just as the guide knows which parts of the city will enrich the visitor's experience, the attention mechanism knows which pieces of information will most enrich the AI's understanding.

In both cases, the essential function is to provide focus, sharpening the deluge of information into a digestible format that can be more readily understood and utilized, whether it's key facts for an exam or must-see landmarks on a trip. It's a process that transforms a scattered array of data points into a coherent thread of knowledge.

Here is the breakdown on the attention mechanism process within a neural network:

- **Initial Input of Data:**


   - Raw data is input into the neural network.

- This could be text, images, or any data that the network is designed to process.

- ## Feature Extraction:

- The network analyzes the raw input to identify features.

- In the context of text, this could include identifying parts of speech or sentence structure.

- ## Calculation of Attention Scores:

- For each element in the input, an attention score is calculated.

- Scores reflect the relevance of each element in relation to the task at hand, such as translating text.

- ## Role of Queries, Keys, and Values:

- **Queries** are representations of the current item being processed.

- **Keys** correspond to the elements in the input sequence that the queries will be compared to.

- **Values** are the actual content from the input sequence that we want to focus on.

- Each query interacts with all keys to create a set of attention scores.

## - Normalization Using Softmax Function:

- The softmax function converts attention scores into probabilities between 0 and 1.

- This process ensures that the attention scores across the input sum to 1.

- It allows the model to probabilistically focus on the most relevant elements.

## - Selective Focus and the Network's Output:

- The normalized attention scores effectively 'weigh' the corresponding values.

- The weighted values are then summed up to become the output for that part of the input.

- This step is analogous to forming a response based on the most pertinent information.

## - Effect on Output (Example - Text Summarization):

- In text summarization, the attention mechanism helps identify the most crucial sentences.

- By focusing on key sentences, the neural network can generate concise, relevant summaries.

- This selects valuable information from a large document while filtering out the noise.

By following these steps, the neural network, armed with an attention mechanism, can perform complex tasks such as summarizing lengthy documents or translating between languages with improved accuracy, showcasing the transformative power of AI in interpreting and utilizing vast amounts of data more like a human would.

Think of a transformer in AI as a well-oiled assembly line of office workers, each with a specific, crucial role in handling a document. As the paper travels down the line, one worker checks for typos, another formats the paragraphs, and yet another polishes the language. Together, their individual contributions ensure that by the time the document reaches the end of the line, it's not just a series of sentences but a coherent, eloquent piece of writing, ready for presentation.

Just like this network of workers, transformers in AI manage streams of data with precision. Each module, or 'worker', specializes in capturing different aspects of the information. Some focus on the context around a particular word, some on the meaning, and others on how words relate to each other across sentences. By the time the data has moved through the transformer, the system has a comprehensive understanding of the text, mirroring the collaborative efficiency of a team of experts.

This process is the bedrock of why transformers are so effective: their ability to orchestrate multiple perspectives leads to a deeper and more sophisticated comprehension of data.

Much as a team of skilled office workers produces superb work, transformers facilitate polished, nuanced AI applications that enrich our daily digital experiences.

Here is the breakdown on the architecture of transformers in AI and how they process data:

- **Input Layer:**

   - Receives the raw data, such as a sentence in the source language for machine translation.

   - Converts words into vectors (numerical representations) that the model can understand.

- **Encoding Process:**

   - Consists of a stack of identical layers that transform the input vector sequence.

   - Each layer includes two main sub-components: a multi-head self-attention mechanism and a simple, position-wise fully connected feed-forward network.

   - Encodes the input data into an intermediate representation that captures the context of each word within the sentence.

- **Self-Attention Mechanism:**

   - Assigns relevance to each word in a sentence compared to

53

others (attention scores).

- Subdivided into multiple 'heads', allowing the model to focus on different parts of the input sentence simultaneously.

- **Normalization and Feed-Forward Network:**

- Applies layer normalization to help stabilize the learning process.

- Processes the attention output to further refine the intermediate representation of the input data.

- **Decoding Process:**

- Mirrors the encoding stack but with additional layers that focus on the encoded input and the output generated so far.

- Includes a multi-head attention mechanism to look at the encoder's output and another to focus on the decoder's own output.

- **Output Layer:**

- Transforms the decoder's output into a sequence of vectors representing the target translation.

- Converts these vectors into actual words in the target language.

- ## Attention Weight Calculation:

- Uses the 'query', 'key', and 'value' vectors derived from the input data.

- Calculates the dot product of the query with all keys and applies a softmax to derive the weights.

- Multiplies the weights with the values to obtain the output of the attention layer.

- ## End-to-End Process Example (Machine Translation):

- The transformer takes a sentence in the source language and translates it into the target language.

- The entire sentence is processed at once, unlike older models that take sequential approaches.

- This leads to faster translations that consider the context of the sentence more effectively.

By utilizing this sophisticated mechanism, transformers can execute tasks like translating sentences with a level of nuance and understanding that closely mimics human language processing. While the technology is complex, each component's role is simple and structured, building up like layers of understanding to produce the final translated text.

Step into the world where Google's BERT and OpenAI's GPT-4 are reshaping how we interact with technology. BERT, which stands for Bidirectional Encoder Representations from Transformers, changes the game in search engines. When you type a query into Google, instead of zeroing in on keywords, BERT's understanding of natural language nuances helps fetch responses that match the query's true intent. It can grasp the significance of prepositions and the context surrounding words, turning a list of search results into answers that feel almost as if they've been hand-picked by a human expert.

On the other side, OpenAI's GPT-4 is revolutionizing text generation. This powerful tool doesn't just write text; it generates rich, coherent content that can mimic a variety of writing styles. From composing emails to drafting articles or even coding, GPT-4 can do it with astonishing accuracy and creativity. Its ability to understand and generate human-like text has the potential to change how we write and create content, offering a level of assistance that was once the stuff of science fiction.

Both BERT and GPT-4 are transformative, making our digital experiences more intuitive and interactive. They represent great strides in AI, pushing the boundaries of how machines understand and respond to human language, enriching user experience in profound and personal ways.

Let's look at the intricacies of BERT and GPT-4, two AI models that have significantly advanced how machines understand and generate human language. Google's BERT is known for its bidirectional processing, a formidable technique that allows the model to consider the full context of a word by looking at the words that come before and after it. Unlike previous models that processed text in only one direction, BERT examines the surrounding words in both directions, creating a richer understanding of language nuances. This bidirectional context is key to BERT's ability to discern the full intent behind search queries, making it a revolutionary tool within search engines.

On the other hand, OpenAI's GPT-4 utilizes an extensive language model with a vast number of parameters, enabling it to produce written content with an impressive range of styles and topics. The size of GPT-4's model and the breadth of its training data allow it to recognize patterns and generate text that is fluid and contextually relevant, from creative fiction to technical code. It's as if GPT-4 has read an immeasurable amount of text and can now emulate the nuances of human communication with precision.

The sophistication of these systems lies in their complex neural network architectures that simulate aspects of human cognition. BERT's attention mechanism and GPT-4's layered approach to processing text represent the forefront of AI's capabilities. They showcase the power of blending vast datasets with intricate algorithms to create AI models that understand language in a way that is transformative for user experience.

Picture a group of colleagues working on a complex project together. Each team member has a different perspective and unique insights into the task. Now, envision the self-attention mechanism in a neural network as this collaborative team. Each 'member' of this mechanism considers the entire input sequence—much like each colleague would consider all aspects of a project—and decides on which part to focus. Just as a team member weighs the significance of their colleague's input to reach the best outcome, each word or data point in a sequence uses self-attention to determine how much it should be influenced by every other word when processing information.

Self-attention allows every element to dynamically adjust its focus, giving precedence to parts that are most relevant for understanding the overall picture, similar to how a strategic team leader might allocate more time to the most impactful aspects of a project. This results in a network that adjusts its attention distribution over the input data, crafting an output that's informed by a comprehensive view rather than isolated snippets. It's not just about computing; it's about grasping context and meaning in a way that mirrors human cooperation and judgement, ensuring AI systems are more intuitive and effective when it comes to tasks like translation, summarization, and beyond.

Let's look at the self-attention mechanism used in neural networks to refine how AI processes information. Picture the input data as a sentence, with each word transformed into a vector—a list of numbers—that encodes its meaning. From these vectors, the self-attention system generates three new types of vectors: queries, keys, and values, much like creating index terms to reference the main points from a book.

Each word's query vector is paired with every other word's key vector to compute attention scores, similar to matching those index terms against every main point to find the best fit. This matching is done using the dot product, a mathematical operation that measures how similar two vectors are. The closer and more aligned the vectors are, the higher the score, denoting the relevance between the words.

As raw attention scores can vary widely, the softmax function comes into play, converting them into probabilities between zero and one. This function ensures the scores for a word sum up to one, like turning raw scores into a percentage, signifying the likelihood of each word's importance in the context of the others.

Next, each value vector gets weighted by these attention probabilities, ensuring that words deemed more relevant have greater influence. Adding up these weighted values gives a new vector that captures the essence of that word within the sentence's context.

Through multiple layers of this mechanism, the neural

network refines its understanding of the input data, much like an editor revising a draft, each layer making it sharper. The result is a sophisticated representation of the original input, poised to improve tasks like translation or question-answering, showcasing how AI's selective focus mimics human cognition.

At the heart of modern AI lie transformers and attention mechanisms, quietly orchestrating a revolution in how we engage with our digital world. These technologies decipher the nuance of language, letting search engines understand our questions with remarkable insight and virtual assistants communicate with a near-human touch. They work behind the scenes, analyzing and responding to our input not just accurately but contextually, often across different languages and tasks.

Looking ahead, these mechanisms are poised to evolve, becoming more adept at interpreting emotions and subtleties in human communication. The potential is there for AI that not only interacts with us but anticipates our needs, offers creative solutions, and performs intricate tasks that today require human enterprise. As these technologies continue to mature, we can expect them to permeate deeper into our daily technology interactions, making them more seamless, intuitive, and, ultimately, more human-like.

# TRAINING LARGE LANGUAGE MODELS

Welcome to the unfolding narrative of Large Language Models (LLMs), where the art of teaching machines to understand and generate human language is pushing the boundaries of what's possible with artificial intelligence. This journey isn't just about creating algorithms; it's about instilling a sense of language in a machine, much the way a skilled teacher nurtures comprehension and expression in a student. As you step through the doors of this exploration, you'll witness how meticulously collected data, when woven through the intricate looms of neural networks, gives birth to systems that can converse, compose, and comprehend. Each chapter of this process, from the initial gathering of vast text corpuses to the rigorous training regimens, contributes to a greater story—one where technology meets linguistics and machines start to speak the language of humans with astonishing coherence. This is a chapter in AI that doesn't just change how machines operate; it transforms how they interact with us in our daily lives, in business, education, and beyond.

At the core of Large Language Models (LLMs) lie three fundamental building blocks: datasets, algorithms, and neural network architectures. Just as you need bricks, mortar, and a blueprint to construct a sturdy building, these three components work together to build robust AI systems that comprehend and use human language.

Beginning with datasets, imagine them as the vast libraries of the digital world. These are collections of written text from a multitude of sources, offering the raw material from which the AI learns language. This can include everything from novels to news articles, ensuring the AI is exposed to varied patterns of language use.

Algorithms are the master craftsmen, the set of rules and instructions that teach the AI how to read through these text collections efficiently, discern patterns, and make connections. Think of them as the process a baker follows to knead and shape dough into bread; they are what guide the LLM to process and understand the data.

Lastly, the neural network architecture is akin to the baker's oven, the structure that holds everything together and transforms the raw ingredients into a finished product. It's the sophisticated design of algorithms and computational layers that allows the AI to not just mimic but understand nuances of language and produce responses that feel natural.

Together, these elements form the bedrock of LLMs, crucial for developing AI that doesn't just mimic speech but engages in meaningful conversation, and reflects their growing prominence in our interaction with technology.

Let's look at the intricate structure of neural network architectures central to Large Language Models, and delve into how each part contributes to their remarkable abilities. First up are the types of layers you might encounter, such as encoders and decoders, especially in transformer-based models like those used in GPT (Generative Pretrained Transformer) series. An encoder layer processes the input data, breaking down and analyzing it, much like the first round of a complex problem-solving task. It's where the network starts to understand the context of the words in the data it's been fed.

In contrast, decoder layers are more about prediction and generation; they take the context understood by the encoder and use it to produce an output, which could be something like the next word in a sentence. The layers communicate through attention mechanisms—think of these as spotlight operators at a play, uniquely focusing on different characters to derive meaning from their dialogues and actions.

Each layer is composed of nodes, or neurons, which are like the brain's workforce—processing information, making connections, and passing along their findings. During training, nodes are activated by functions that decide how much of the learned information to pass on; much like people making decisions based on their knowledge and experience.

Now, for these networks to 'learn', they use a process known as backpropagation. This is the network's way of learning from mistakes and successes, akin to self-reflection. By cycling through examples over and over, and adjusting their inner parameters accordingly, the networks gradually learn to produce more accurate results.

This is just the tip of the iceberg when it comes to the sophistication of these architectures. They are marvels of computational science, marrying mathematics and technology to give machines a whisper of human-like understanding and expression.

Imagine a chef poised to create a culinary masterpiece, standing amidst the bustle of a fresh market. With trained eyes, the chef selects an array of ingredients: herbs rich with aroma, vegetables vibrant in color, and proteins of the finest quality. Each choice is deliberate, aimed at achieving a balance of flavors on the plate. Now, compare this to training Large Language Models (LLMs) – the data is the recipe's ingredients. Just as the quality of a meal hinges on the freshness and caliber of its components, the success of LLMs depends on the quality of data they consume.

Data serves as the sustenance from which LLMs learn the intricacies of language, its subtle rules and vibrant variations. Feeding an LLM poor data is akin to serving gourmet diners a dish made of wilted produce and stale spices – the result is subpar. Thus, sourcing the best data, rich and diverse in context and style, becomes the chef's – and AI developer's – most crucial task. This ensures that, like a well-crafted dish leaving a lasting impression, the LLM can generate text that is coherent, relevant, and, quite simply, a delight to the end-user's proverbial palate.

Here is the breakdown on the varied types of data used in training Large Language Models:

- **Literary Texts:**

  - Novels, short stories, and poetry that provide nuanced use of language and a wealth of vocabulary.

  - Importance: Crucial for teaching the models rich language and diverse narrative styles.

- **Dialogues:**

  - Conversations from plays, movies, and transcripts that teach the flow of natural speech.

  - Importance: Helps the model understand conversational language and colloquialisms.

- **Technical Documents:**

  - Academic papers, manuals, and reports that contain

specialized terminology and structured information.

- Importance: Essential for training models to comprehend and generate industry-specific language.

- **Social Media Content:**

- Posts, comments, and messages that highlight current slang, abbreviations, and informal dialogue.

- Importance: Makes the model adept at recognizing and engaging with contemporary and informal language.

- **Quality of Data:**

- Accurate, well-written sources that are free from errors and represent broad language diversity.

- Importance: High quality data ensures reliability and decreases the chance of learning incorrect or biased patterns.

- **Variety and Balance:**

- A mix of data sources ensures a comprehensive understanding of language.

- Importance: Prevents the model from being over-specialized in one style or genre.

- **Preprocessing Steps:**

- **Tokenization:**

- Breaking down text into smaller pieces or 'tokens' that the model can easily process.

- Importance: Ensures consistency in how words and phrases are understood by the model.

- **Annotation:**

- Marking data with notes that explain context, sentiments, or grammar use.

- Importance: Helps the model learn the underlying context and sentiment behind language.

- **Normalization:**

- Standardizing text to reduce complexity, such as converting to one case or expanding abbreviations.

- Importance: Aids in the uniform processing of language and reduces noise in the data.

Each component is a thread in the tapestry of language understanding that LLMs aim to weave. By meticulously selecting and crafting data, researchers can provide a solid dataset from which language models can learn effectively, preparing them to handle the vast and complex landscapes of human communication.

Just as there are countless ways to design a building, there is a variety of architectures in the creation of AI models, each with strategic designs catering to specific functions. Consider the classic design of a bungalow, simplistic yet functional for comfortable living; this can be likened to a feedforward neural network - straightforward, and ideal for basic tasks. Now, picture a skyscraper, reaching towards the sky with its complexity and scale; it's akin to a deep learning network, layered with intricacies and capable of handling a myriad of operations.

Take, for instance, the contrast between a cobblestone cottage and a sleek glass-fronted office building. The former, with its thick walls and quaint windows, offers a sturdy, if not particularly flexible, structure resembling early machine learning models with limited parameters. Meanwhile, the latter's expansive windows and open-plan floors embody the adaptability and extensive connectivity of transformer models, capable of focusing on different data points much like office workers collaborate across an open space.

Each architectural choice in buildings serves a purpose, from the grandeur of a cathedral, orchestrating light and sound, to the efficiency of a warehouse, maximizing space and utility. Similarly, the structure of an AI model's architecture dictates its functionality, whether it's sorting through data, recognizing speech patterns, or translating languages. The foundation, pillars, and materials may vary, but the intent remains the same: to create something purposeful, effective, and suited to meet specific needs, illuminating how carefully constructed forms — in buildings or in AI — can house remarkable capabilities.

Here is the breakdown on different AI neural network architectures:

- ## Recurrent Neural Networks (RNN):

- **Purpose:** Optimized for processing sequential data such as time series or language.

- **Layers:** Composed of loops within neural network cells that allow information to be carried across sequence steps.

- **Nodes:** Typically include memory cells that maintain information over time.

- ## Functions:

- Recognizing patterns in sequences.

- Generating text or speech.

- Speech recognition applications due to their temporal dynamic behavior.

- **Impact:** RNNs can struggle with long-term dependencies, but they excel in tasks where context is closely linked, like chatbots or time series forecasting.

- ## Convolutional Neural Networks (CNN):

- **Purpose:** Efficient for spatial data processing, such as image and video recognition.

- **Layers:** Feature convolutional layers that filter inputs for useful information, pooling layers that reduce dimensionality, and fully connected layers for classification.

- **Nodes:** Convolutional nodes apply filters to localized input regions and pooling nodes that summarize the features.

- **Functions:**

  - Image classification.

  - Facial recognition systems.

  - Analyzing visual data of all kinds.

- **Impact:** CNNs perform well in identifying patterns in space, so they're used where visual patterns are critical, successfully powering image recognition and classification tasks.

- **Transformers:**

- **Purpose:** Designed to handle ordered sequences of data like those found in natural language.

- **Layers:** Consist of encoder layers to process the input text and decoder layers to generate the output text, utilizing multi-head self-attention mechanisms.

- **Nodes:** Attention nodes weight input differently, allowing focus on relevant parts of data.

- **Functions:**

  - Translating between languages.

  - Summarizing large pieces of text.

  - Generating readable and contextually relevant content.

- **Impact:** Transformers circumvent the limitations of RNNs by processing entire sequences of data simultaneously, which is why they have become the go-to architecture for tasks like language translation and content generation.

Each architecture embodies a specific approach to processing data, reflecting sophisticated strategies designed to overcome the challenges inherent to different AI tasks. The choice of architecture, layers, and nodes has a profound effect on the machine's performance, much like selecting the right materials and designs is crucial in constructing buildings fit for their purpose. These neural networks, with their unique architectures, pave the way for advancements in AI that are becoming increasingly central to technological growth and everyday life.

Training a Large Language Model (LLM) is like coaching an athlete - systematic and incremental. First, we start with a clear goal: to process and generate human-like language. Here's a step-by-step on how it's done.

The coach, or AI trainer, begins by gathering a comprehensive set of training materials, akin to an athlete's balanced diet. For an LLM, this 'diet' is a vast dataset full of text from books, articles, and websites. This data is prepared and cleaned, much like peeling and chopping vegetables, to ensure it's 'digestible' for the model.

Once the data is ready, the real training kicks off. The LLM wades through this sea of information, looking for patterns and learning the nuances of language - this is its workout routine. It makes a lot of mistakes initially, but each error is an opportunity for learning. The model predicts a piece of text, compares it with the correct 'answer', and adjusts its internal parameters slightly to be more accurate the next time. It's akin to a runner adjusting their stride or a golfer correcting their swing.

This routine is repeated with millions, sometimes billions, of examples. Over time, just as muscles adapt with exercise, the LLM becomes increasingly proficient at producing and understanding language. It learns not just vocabulary and grammar but also context, style, and even subtlety. At the end of this rigorous training process, just as an athlete stands ready at the starting block, the LLM is prepared to tackle real-world tasks, from translating languages to helping you write an email.

Each phase of the training is carefully monitored and adjusted, making sure that the LLM doesn't just memorize its 'diet', but truly understands the language it 'consumes'. With the right coaching, LLMs can become versatile linguists, connecting with us across the digital space in ways that are ever more seamless and intuitive.

Let's look at the detailed process of training Large Language Models and demystify the algorithms that make it possible. At the core of training, we have what's known as a loss function, typically cross-entropy loss for LLMs. This function acts like a scoring system. It calculates the difference between the model's predictions and the actual expected outcomes — essentially measuring how 'wrong' a model's language predictions are at any given step.

To improve performance, just like a coach adjusts an athlete's technique, the LLM uses optimization algorithms like stochastic gradient descent or its more sophisticated cousin, the Adam optimizer. These algorithms work by minutely adjusting the weight of connections within the model to decrease the loss score over numerous training rounds.

During backpropagation, the model looks back at its errors, distributes responsibility across its architecture, and learns how to adjust its internal parameters. Think of it as a game of 'hotter-colder' where the model is guided to 'warmer' areas of more correct language responses.

Preventing overfitting, where a model performs well on its training data but can't generalize to new data, is crucial. Validation sets are like surprise quizzes that check if the model is truly understanding the material or just memorizing it. If the model only performs well on previously seen data, it's time to tweak the training with techniques like dropout, which can be likened to cross-training that prevents the model from relying too heavily on any single pattern.

Finally, learning rate schedules adjust the magnitude of updates to the model's weights. In simpler terms, they control how quickly the model learns from new data at different stages of training. Initially, larger learning steps are taken to make gross improvements, and over time, these adjustments become finer, refining the model's understanding.

Through meticulous adjustments and constant evaluation, LLMs learn to grasp and generate nuanced human language. This process reflects not just a triumph of programming but a choreographed dance of mathematical principles that underlie modern AI, enabling machines to communicate in ways once confined to the realms of imagination.

Training large-scale AI models is a bit like running a mega-factory—it requires immense computational power and speed, which poses significant challenges. The sheer amount of data these models must learn from demands robust and efficient hardware, akin to needing a fast assembly line to produce cars in a plant.

To meet these challenges, the field relies on graphical processing units (GPUs) and tensor processing units (TPUs), which are like specialized tools on the assembly line, designed to handle specific tasks more efficiently than traditional tools. These processing units accelerate the mathematical calculations necessary for training AI, much like how power tools speed up production on an assembly line.

Distributing the computing workload is another approach, reminiscent of dividing tasks among multiple workers. This is done through parallel processing and cloud computing, which together ensure that the heavy lifting of data analysis doesn't overwhelm a single machine, allowing for faster, more efficient model training.

Moreover, sophisticated software frameworks optimize these hardware capabilities. They manage the workflow and instructions for the processors, just as a foreman oversees and directs assembly line workers to ensure everything runs smoothly.

By leveraging such technologies, the field of AI overcomes computational hurdles, making it possible to train models that can analyze vast datasets and perform tasks beyond the scope of unaided human intellect. This panorama of computational architecture and strategy ensures that AI continues to grow smarter, better, and faster, transforming what we can achieve with technology.

```
// Pseudocode for training an AI model
// Step 1: Initialize model parameters

model = initialize_model()

// Step 2: Load and prepare data

data = load_data('training_dataset')

prepared_data = preprocess_data(data)

// Begin training over several iterations, called epochs

for epoch in range(number_of_epochs):

    // Step 3: Process data in small batches

    for batch in split_into_batches(prepared_data, batch_size):

        // Step 4: Forward propagation

        predictions = model.forward_propagate(batch.inputs)

        // Step 5: Compute loss

        loss = compute_loss(predictions, batch.targets)

        // Step 6: Backpropagation to calculate gradients

        gradients = model.backpropagate(loss)

        // Step 7: Update model weights

        model.update_weights(gradients, learning_rate)

// Programming GPUs and TPUs for tensor operations

// GPUs and TPUs have parallel architectures that allow faster matrix and vector operations

gpu_result = gpu_device.perform_tensor_operations(tensor_data)


tpu_result = tpu_device.perform_tensor_operations(tensor_data)

// Parallel processing across CPUs, GPUs, or TPUs for large datasets
```

```
parallel_results    =    parallel_compute(cluster_devices,    'tensor_operations',
large_dataset)

// Setting up cloud environments for distributed computing

cloud_environment = setup_cloud(resource_allocation, storage_capacity)

deploy_model_to_cloud(model, cloud_environment)

// Software frameworks managing tasks and resource allocation

framework = load_framework('TensorFlow or PyTorch')

framework.manage_resources(hardware_devices)

framework.allocate_tasks(data_loading, model_training, model_evaluation)

// Wrap-up
// The above steps are iterated over, with each epoch the model improves
// The weights, biases, and other parameters are adjusted
// Through frameworks like TensorFlow or PyTorch, which abstract low-level
operations
// Distributed computing in the cloud allows scaling up the training
// GPUs and TPUs provide the computational power needed for rapid tensor
calculations
// The end goal is a well-trained model, capable of generalizing beyond the training
data
```

This narrative and pseudocode give you a glimpse into the precise steps and tools involved in the computational process of machine learning. It illustrates how model parameters are initiated and refined through cycles of forward and backward passes, making use of the parallel computing powers of GPUs and TPUs. It also shows how large datasets are managed and how cloud technologies streamline the process for scale and efficiency. The software frameworks serve as the 'conductors' for these complex 'orchestras,' ensuring every 'instrument' plays its part to create harmonious AI 'symphonies'.

The training of Large Language Models (LLMs) carries with it ethical considerations much like society adheres to specific laws and norms to function harmoniously. Just as traffic laws were established to ensure safe and orderly travel as cars became ubiquitous, ethical standards in AI seek to prevent harm and misuse as technology becomes an integral part of our lives. As LLMs learn and grow from the data they process, it's vital to ensure that this data doesn't perpetuate biases or false information, much like how civic planning strives to create inclusive and safe urban spaces for all citizens.

Looking forward, we can draw parallels between the evolution of transportation and the development of LLMs. The transition from horse-drawn carriages to self-driving cars mirrors the trajectory from basic programming to autonomous LLMs capable of nuanced understanding and creation. Just as modern vehicles are equipped with safety features and navigation systems that were once unimagined, future LLMs may possess sophisticated self-regulation mechanisms to ensure ethical considerations are seamlessly integrated into their operation. These advancements in LLMs will potentially streamline vast portions of our digital experience, making information exchange and content creation more efficient, much like how bullet trains shortened travel times between distant cities. With careful navigation of their ethical landscape, LLMs have the potential to drive society to new horizons of connectivity and understanding.

Here is the breakdown on the ethical considerations in LLM training:

- **Fairness:**

- **Bias Detection:**

    - Analyze training data for imbalances and skewness.

    - Implement checks to identify language patterns that may

disadvantage any group.

### - Bias Correction:

- Create more balanced datasets by including diverse sources of text.

- Adjust model algorithms to discount biased data points.

### - Privacy:

### - Data Anonymization:

- Strip out personally identifiable information from datasets.

- Use synthetic data generated to ensure privacy while still providing realistic training material.

### - Data Usage Protocols:

- Establish clear rules for what data can be used for training.

- Enforce strict access controls and encryption for stored data.

### - Inclusivity:

- **Representation in Data:**

  - Incorporate text in multiple languages and dialects.

  - Ensure datasets reflect a variety of cultural and social perspectives.

- **Design for Diversity:**

  - Involve diverse teams in the development and review of AI models.

  - Continuously monitor model outputs for indications of exclusivity or insensitivity.

- **Speculation on Future Mechanisms:**

- **Automated Ethical Audits:**

  - Develop systems within LLMs to regularly assess the fairness of their language processing, akin to self-diagnostic tools in vehicles.

- **Adaptation and Learning:**

  - Equip LLMs with the ability to adapt over time to changing societal norms and values, similar to how navigation systems update with the latest maps and regulations.

Each of these components plays a crucial role in upholding ethical standards that are aligned with societal values. Just as automobiles now come equipped with technology to detect potential hazards and protect passengers, it's conceivable that LLMs of the future will be designed with built-in ethical safeguards to prevent harm and endorse a more inclusive digital society. Understanding these minute yet critical aspects demystifies the responsible creation and implementation of LLMs in a world where AI is becoming more omnipresent.

In this chapter, we explored the intricate process of training Large Language Models (LLMs). Starting from collecting and preparing diverse datasets to the sophisticated dance of algorithms fine-tuning a model's understanding of language, we peeled back the layers of this sophisticated technology. We unraveled how these AI powerhouses are schooled to process information in batches, learning from each interaction and gradually sharpening their linguistic abilities like an artist refining their craft.

Diving further, we recognized the colossal computational might behind LLMs, made possible by advanced hardware and smartly distributed processing, ensuring their seamless operation without overwhelming any single system. We were also confronted with the gravity of ethical considerations, drawing parallels to societal laws and norms that guide behavior and advancements, like those in transportation, that have informed the design of roadways and vehicles for safer, more efficient travel.

LLMs have firmly taken their place as cornerstones in AI progress, shaping the way we interact with digital entities. Looking beyond mere text generation, their potential ventures into realms of nuanced communication and understanding, creating a bridge between human thought and machine intelligence. The impact of these models is as broad as the society itself, touching everything from daily conveniences to profound changes in how we work and learn. As we continue on this journey with LLMs, it's clear they are not just tools but partners in sculpting a new era of technology that responds, reflects, and enhances the human experience.

# UNDERSTANDING LLMS TEXT GENERATION

Next up is the captivating world of LLMs' text generation, where the wonders of artificial intelligence meet the elegance of human language. Picture a realm where machines not only understand the subtleties of our words but can also craft sentences as though they were skilled writers themselves. In this chapter, we unravel how Large Language Models learn to spin narratives, compose poetry, and even simulate conversation, all through the seemingly magical process of AI training. From their initial 'lessons' in language to their proficient written masterpieces, these models represent a leap in how we interact with technology, paving the way for innovations that once lived only in the imagination. As you journey through these pages, you'll gain insights into not just the 'how' but also the 'why' behind this groundbreaking technology, making each complex idea clear and approachable. Whether a curious newcomer or an informed enthusiast, you're in for an exploration that's as enlightening as it is exciting. Join in as we unfold the story of how machines are learning to speak our language.

The building blocks of any Large Language Model's education start with its diet of data: the more substantial and nutritious this data, the better the model will become at crafting text. Just as a well-rounded diet is vital for a person's health, the diversity and quality of data are crucial for the robust development of an LLM.

These models feed on vast libraries of text—books, articles, conversations, web pages—each piece contributing to the LLM's understanding of human language. Quantity is important because it ensures exposure to the many ways we communicate, from poetic expressions to everyday banter. However, quality cannot be overlooked. Accurate, representative, and carefully vetted data are akin to selecting the finest ingredients for a meal: they ensure the model learns to replicate and innovate upon language that is both rich and free from inadvertent biases.

The treatment of this data matters too. Much like cleaning and prepping ingredients before cooking, datasets are meticulously cleaned and transformed into formats that the LLM can digest and learn from efficiently. The result is an AI master chef in text generation, knowledgeable in a wide array of linguistic styles and capable of producing sentences that echo the depth and diversity of human expression.

Let's look at the meticulous steps involved in prepping data for training Large Language Models, akin to a chef preparing their ingredients before the actual cooking begins.

First comes the cleaning process. Just as one might rinse vegetables to remove dirt, data cleaning involves stripping text of anything that's not useful for learning—irrelevant formatting, erroneous characters, and redundant information are removed to prevent the model from learning unnecessary patterns.

Normalization is the next step, where different forms of the same word, like "isn't" and "is not," are standardized. Think of it as organizing ingredients into uniform portions before combining them into a dish, ensuring consistent taste in every bite.

Tokenization breaks down chunks of text into smaller pieces, much like chopping ingredients so they blend better. By dividing text into words or even smaller units like subwords, models learn the granularity of language, making them adept at assembling it back together in novel ways.

Vectorization then turns these tokens into numerical values that the LLM can process. In the culinary analogy, this is like measuring out precise quantities of each ingredient. These numbers capture the essence of words, their meaning, and context, which the model uses to cook up new text sequences.

To remove biases—akin to removing allergens from a dish so that everyone can enjoy it—datasets undergo careful examination. Patterns that could introduce unfair biases or stereotypes are identified and reduced, aiming to craft language models that generate text fair and representative of diverse voices.

Automating these tasks is crucial for handling the vast amounts of data LLMs require, akin to a commercial kitchen using food processors over hand-cutting. This automation frees up time, increases consistency, and makes complex language tasks manageable, a crucial ingredient to developing language models that comprehend and mirror the intricacies of human communication.

By understanding these behind-the-scenes efforts, one gains a deeper appreciation for how LLMs learn from data and why their foundations must be as solid and unbiased as possible, ensuring the text they generate is both meaningful and comprehensible.

At the heart of a Large Language Model lies a cleverly constructed architecture made up of encoders, decoders, and self-attention mechanisms. One can liken the encoder to a diligent note-taker, carefully listening to a story; it meticulously analyzes and understands the input text, organizing the information much like bullet points in preparation for a presentation.

The decoder then acts as the presenter, taking the gathered points and transforming them into a compelling narrative. It picks up where the encoder left off, generating a coherent output that could be the next line in a poem or an answer to a question, akin to delivering the speech in a way that captivates the audience.

The magic ingredient that enhances the working of these two components is the self-attention mechanism. This aspect allows the model to look at the input text strategically, focusing on important words and phrase connections as needed, much as a crafty narrator changes their tone and inflection to emphasize critical parts of a tale.

Together, these components enable the LLM to not only process and understand chunks of text but also create new content that reads as if a knowledgeable author had carefully composed it. This is how machines are equipped with the power to mesmerize readers, capturing the complexities and subtleties of human language with remarkable precision. It's a process that's transforming interactions with technology, making the leap from mechanical responses to engaging, dynamic dialogue.

In the world of Large Language Models, the encoder, decoder, and self-attention mechanisms work together to process and generate human-like text. Here's a step-by-step guide to unravel their roles and functionalities.

The encoder is essentially the model's comprehension unit. It takes the input text and breaks it down into understandable pieces. Like an expert linguist, it examines the text to capture its meaning and nuances. Inside the encoder are layers, each adding to the depth of understanding by encoding the text into higher-level representations.

Now, for each layer within the encoder, there's a parallel layer in the decoder. The decoder's job is to take the processed information from the encoder and turn it into new text. Picture a translator who listens to a speaker before translating the speech into another language; that's what the decoder does, creating text that's a coherent continuation or response to the input.

Self-attention, a component within these layers, allows the model to weigh the importance of different words in a sentence. Imagine being in a conversation and focusing more on certain words to grasp the speaker's true intent—that's what self-attention does. It helps the model decide which words are most relevant in understanding and generating language.

The term 'multi-head' in self-attention refers to the model's ability to pay attention to different parts of the sentence simultaneously. It's akin to having multiple experts analyzing a complex problem at once, each bringing their unique perspective, resulting in a more comprehensive solution.

These finely-tuned mechanisms within encoder and decoder layers, empowered by sophisticated self-attention, make LLMs not just proficient in language but also in capturing the diversity of contexts within human communication. This intricate dance of computational processes reflects the sophistication of LLM architectures, laying the foundation for AI systems that communicate with an understanding that edges ever closer to human intellect.

Training a Large Language Model to grasp and generate language involves a multi-stage process, each phase building upon the last to refine the model's linguistic abilities. It begins with the initial training phase, where the model is exposed to massive amounts of text - this is where it starts to learn language patterns, much like a child learns to speak by listening to the conversations around them.

Patterns such as word order, grammar, and common phrases

become ingrained during this stage, laying a foundational understanding of how language works. This phase is critical, as it sets the stage for the more nuanced understanding that comes later.

Once the basics are in place, the model enters the fine-tuning phase. Here, specific data sets, often relevant to particular tasks or industries, are used to teach the LLM the subtle differences and intricacies of language use. It's comparable to an apprentice shadowing a master craftsman, picking up the refined skills and nuances of the trade.

This fine-tuning is not just about adding more vocabulary; it's about teaching the LLM to understand context, tone, implied meanings, and cultural nuances – the subtle aspects that give human communication its richness and depth.

Through repeated cycles of prediction and correction, the LLM hones its language generation capabilities, striving to mimic the complexity and subtlety of human writers. It's a meticulous and ongoing process, but one that endows these models with the remarkable ability to produce text that resonates with human readers on a deeper level.

Here is the breakdown on the stages and computational processes involved in LLM training:

- **Initial Data Feeding Phase:**

- **Dataset Curation:**

- Collection: Gathering text from diverse sources such as literature, websites, and transcriptions to ensure a wide range of language use.

- Filtering: Removing inappropriate or irrelevant content to maintain model integrity and relevance.

## - Preprocessing Techniques:

- Tokenization: Splitting text into tokens (words or subwords) for the model to analyze.

- Normalization: Converting text to a uniform style, like lowercasing and expanding contractions for consistency.

- Vectorization: Turning tokens into numerical values so the LLM can process them mathematically.

## - Fine-Tuning Stage:

## - Specialized Datasets:

- Utilizing topic-specific texts to adapt the model's output to particular fields or applications.

## - User Feedback Integration:

- Collecting user interactions to adjust the model's understanding and generation of language.

## - Algorithms for Contextual Understanding:

- Implementing attention mechanisms allowing the LLM to weigh the importance of each part of the input when creating output.

- **Iterative Process of Performance Evaluation:**

- **Test Suites:**

- Employing a set of language tasks to gauge the model's proficiency and identify areas needing improvement.

- **Reinforcement Learning:**

- Using algorithms that enable the model to learn from its success and mistakes, refining its responses over time.

Each of these components plays a vital role in sharpening the language model's ability to not just understand, but also to generate text that feels as natural and nuanced as something a human might write. From the selection and preparation of data to the methodical tuning and continuous advancement of its language faculties, an LLM's training is a complex yet remarkably structured sequence of stages, each contributing to the model's growing acumen. In understanding these parts, one gains a clear view of how we guide machines to navigate the rich terrain of human language.

Imagine a jazz musician, saxophone in hand, standing under a single spotlight. The melody begins, familiar and comfortable, but as the room's energy builds, the musician diverges, embarking on an improvisational journey. This is the essence of a Large Language Model crafting text: it starts with a base—

thematic material similar to a standard tune—and then, drawing on the vast repertoire learned in practice, the model deftly weaves together words and phrases.

Each word is a note, and phrases are melodic lines, selected not at random but with intention and artistry, based on patterns absorbed during training. With every flourish and intricate run of notes, the musician—much like the language model—demonstrates an understanding of both the rules of music and when to bend them for effect.

The parallels run deep, right down to the nod of approval from fellow band members—akin to the validation processes that check whether the generated text harmonizes with what's expected. Just as improvisation showcases a musician's expertise and feel for the craft, text generation is a testament to an LLM's advanced understanding of language, captivating readers note by note, or in this case, word by word.

Here is the breakdown on the technical steps Large Language Models go through to learn and generate human-like text:

- **Collection and Preprocessing of Training Data:**


- Gathering Texts: Accumulating diverse text sources like books, websites, and articles.


- Data Cleaning: Removing irrelevant content, such as headers or footers, and fixing errors.


- Tokenization: Breaking down text into smaller pieces for the model to analyze, like words or sentences.

- Normalization: Standardizing text data, for example, by making all letters lowercase.

### - Initial Training Phase:

- Pattern Recognition: The model learns how language components fit together; for instance, how subjects tend to precede verbs in English.

- Neural Network Weights: Initial adjustments to the model's internal settings based on the recognized patterns.

- Loss Calculation: Computing the difference between the model's output and the correct output to guide improvements.

### - Fine-Tuning for Specific Contexts or Styles:

- Tailored Datasets: Introducing topic-specific texts to adapt the model to specialized language use.

- Contextual Adaptation: Adjusting the model to handle different tones and styles, ensuring it can generate text suitable for various situations.

### - Text Generation Algorithms:

- Keyword and Sequence Decisions: Determining which words to use and their order based on learned patterns.

- Probabilistic Modeling: Using statistical methods to

predict the next word in a sentence.

- Sampling Strategies: Techniques like beam search to consider several possible next words before choosing one.

## - Reinforcement Learning and Backpropagation:

- Parameter Adjustment: Fine-tuning the model's internal parameters when the generated text doesn't match the expected text.

- Continuous Learning: Allowing the model to learn from new data so it can improve over time, akin to lifelong learning in humans.

These steps together enable the LLM to not only understand text input but also to create new, coherent text that often feels like it was written by a human. Just as each note in a melody plays a distinct role but ultimately contributes to a harmonious tune, each technical step in LLM training serves a purpose in the larger task of human-like text generation.

Imagine setting out on a voyage across the sea, armed only with a map and a compass. The compass serves a crucial role, keeping the ship on course, steadfast towards the intended destination, never swaying despite the changing winds and tides. This is akin to implementing ethical guidelines in the deployment of Large Language Models. Just as a navigator uses a compass to steer clear of hazardous routes and remain true to a charted course, developers embed ethical standards into LLMs to ensure that, as they navigate the vast ocean of language, they steer away from harmful outputs and align with the moral values we uphold.

These ethical guidelines work under the hood, often invisible to the end-user, yet they are omnipresent, guiding the LLM's every response, much like a compass quietly influencing the helm's direction. By adhering to these principles, the LLMs maintain a trajectory that respects privacy, prevents biases, and promotes fairness, ensuring the technology enriches society without veering off course into the troubling waters of ethical dilemma. Thus, these guidelines are not just rules but beacons that light the path forward, pivotal in the broader context of responsibly harnessing the winds of AI innovation.

Here is the breakdown on the ethical guidelines for Large Language Models and how they're put into practice, ensuring their deployment aligns with the highest moral standards:

- **Ethical Framework Principles:**

- **Transparency:**

   - Clearly communicating the LLM's capabilities and limitations to users.

   - Documenting and sharing the data sources and training methods used in LLM development.

- **Accountability:**

   - Establishing clear lines of responsibility for the LLM's outputs.

   - Implementing mechanisms for reporting and

addressing misuse or harmful consequences.

## - User Consent:

- Obtaining explicit permission from users for data collection and usage.

- Ensuring users are informed about how their data contributes to LLM training and outputs.

## - Fairness:

- Actively seeking diverse data sets to avoid perpetuating biases.

- Developing models that address and serve the needs of a broad spectrum of society.

## - Bias Assessment and Correction:

## - External Audits:

- Engaging third-party experts to assess the LLM for biases regularly.

## - Feedback Loops:

- Incorporating user feedback to identify and correct

unintended biases in the model.

## - Role of Ethics Committees:

## - Policy Development:

- Formulating guidelines and practices that steer LLM development in ethical directions.

## - Review and Oversight:

- Assessing new features, updates, and data sets for ethical implications before deployment.

## - Continuous Monitoring:

## - Automated Systems:

- Using software tools to monitor the LLM's outputs in real-time for signs of biases or ethical lapses.

## - Human Oversight:

- Having a dedicated team to review flagged content and make context-specific decisions.

## - Updates to Ethical Guidelines:

## - Keeping Pace with Society:

- Regularly updating ethical standards to reflect changing societal values and norms.

## - Technology Advancements:

- Incorporating new research findings and technological capabilities into ethical considerations.

Through this meticulous ethical scaffolding, Large Language Models are deployed not just with cognitive intelligence but also with a moral compass. By detailing these components, it becomes clear how crucial—and complex—the task of embedding ethics in AI truly is. It's about creating models that not only perform tasks but also do so while preserving human dignity and fostering trust.

Just as vehicles have evolved from simple horse-drawn carriages to self-driving cars equipped with an array of sensors and software, Large Language Models are on a trajectory that could take them from basic text predictors to sophisticated companions in our daily digital interactions. Picture this transformation like the shift from manual gears to automatic transmission, which made driving more accessible to the masses. LLMs might soon integrate so seamlessly into our routines that interacting with digital assistants becomes as intuitive as conversing with a friend.

These advanced models could enhance storytelling, introducing a new era where AI doesn't just suggest the next sentence in a story but helps to weave complex narratives with branching plot lines, adjustable to the reader's whims, much like a car that automatically adapts its route in real time based on traffic conditions. The future promises an LLM that not only understands our requests but anticipates our needs and enriches our experiences, expanding the realms of creativity and personalization in the stories we tell and share.

Let's look at the advancements in Large Language Models (LLMs) and the technical foundations that are poised to revolutionize our interaction with digital worlds:

- ### Natural Language Understanding (NLU):

- Enhancements in semantic analysis to grasp the meaning beyond words.

- Advanced sentiment analysis to detect and respond to emotional cues.

- ### Context Awareness:

- Development of memory mechanisms that allow LLMs to retain and apply past interactions to current context.

- The improved coherence of long-form content generation, enabling consistent storytelling over time.

- ### Machine Learning Algorithms:

- Deep learning techniques for pattern recognition within language structures at scale.

- Neural network optimization for faster and more efficient

processing of complex linguistic data.

- **User Intent Prediction:**

- Integration of predictive analytics to anticipate a user's needs and tailor responses.

- Leveraging user behavior data to fine-tune LLM responses for increased relevance.

- **Content Generation for Narrative Structures:**

- Algorithms designed to understand plot development and character arcs.

- Customizable modules for different genres and storytelling styles.

- **Personalized Interaction:**

- User profiling to provide tailored content and interaction experiences.

- Adaptive learning from each user interaction to continuously improve the personalization.

- **Emerging Technologies:**

- **Reinforcement Learning (RL):**

- RL models for dynamic adaptation based on user feedback and engagements.

### - Federated Learning:

- Distributed model training approaches to enhance privacy and utilize decentralized data.

By undressing the technicality of these advances, it's possible to see how LLMs will become more than just tools; they will be partners in creating and narrating stories, offering bespoke experiences that resonate on a personal level. This next chapter in AI development promises a fusion of human creativity and machine intelligence, where the digital narratives we engage with are as dynamic and diverse as our imaginations.

Understanding the world of Large Language Models (LLMs) and their text generation is akin to following the growth of a sapling into a towering tree. It begins with the roots, the vast and varied data from which LLMs draw their sustenance, parsing through language in all its complexity to form a foundational understanding. As they grow, these models, like trees, stretch upwards, expanding in their capabilities and intricacy.

At each layer—from recognizing the patterns of language to the fine-tuning that hones their generation of text—LLMs become more adept. They begin to not only replicate but also innovate, crafting phrases that resonate with seemingly intuitive understanding. And just as a mature tree provides shelter and sustenance, LLMs offer new ways to interact, bringing forth a blossoming landscape where technology and communication converge.

As we peer into the potential future of LLMs, it is clear that their branches may reach even further into our daily lives, providing shade that cools and fruit that nourishes. Their impact is vast, enriching the way we exchange information, share stories, and connect with one another. Through our continued learning and refinement of these models, the promise of AI becomes not just a tool we use, but a companion that enhances the human experience, growing ever more integrated with the rhythms of our life.

# NATURAL LANGUAGE UNDERSTANDING

Get ready to understand about analyzing the ability of LLMs to comprehend context and semantics in various linguistic tasks. It's quite a sight to see how the strings of text we use to express thoughts, tell stories, and convey ideas are now within the grasp of what we know as computers. Here, we'll unravel the curtain to reveal how these machines, powered by Large Language Models, are learning the art of human speech. Each sentence and phrase, to them, is a puzzle they're learning to put together, not just word by word, but with an understanding of meaning and intent akin to our own. It's a process that's as intriguing as it is vital, bridging the gap between human creativity and computational prowess. So settle in, and let's explore this thrilling intersection of technology and language, where complexities are made clear, and the marvels of AI's linguistic capabilities come to life.

Large Language Models function similarly to a meticulous note-taker at a meeting. As you chat, they keep track of the topics discussed, noting down keywords and phrases that serve as anchors for the conversation. They use a kind of digital short-term memory which holds onto the context of what's been said. This ensures that responses are not only relevant but also connected to the ongoing dialogue. Think of it as a careful listener who nods along, remembers your earlier points, and weaves them into the conversation as it progresses. By maintaining this thread of context, LLMs can provide answers and information that make sense within the flow of interaction, offering a conversational experience that feels surprisingly human.

In Large Language Models, 'digital short-term memory' is crucial for understanding and generating coherent dialogue. This memory comes into play through attention mechanisms, which work like a spotlight, highlighting important parts of the conversation that need to be remembered for context.

When a model processes text, it first breaks it down into tokens, much like splitting a sentence into individual words. Each token is then transformed into a numerical form known as an embedding, which captures not just the word itself but its meaning in relation to the other words around it.

Inside the model, neural network layers, which you can think of as a series of processing filters, analyze these embeddings. The attention mechanism assigns weights to each token, determining their importance relative to each other in the given context. Higher-weighted tokens take precedence, as they're likely crucial to the ongoing conversation.

As the model is trained with vast amounts of text, it undergoes countless gradient updates. These updates fine-tune the model's parameters, improving its ability to pick out and remember details that keep the conversation flowing naturally.

This step-by-step flow of tokenization, embedding, attention-weight assignment, and continuous training constitutes the LLM's aptitude for retaining dialogue context, akin to how a storyteller remembers key plot points to construct a captivating tale.

Large Language Models are like keen detectives of language: they look for clues in text to understand its full meaning. To do this, they study the subtle ways words interact, much like analyzing body language and tone in a conversation. These models assess nuances, detect the sentiment, and unravel complex structures through a variety of linguistic cues and patterns. They don't just read text; they interpret it, considering context and the various shades of meaning words can have depending on their placement and use. Through this careful analysis, LLMs deduce intent, making educated guesses about what's being communicated, whether it's a factual statement, a question, or even sarcasm. This ability doesn't just happen; it's a result of intricate programming and layers of neural networks working together to mimic the human capacity for language comprehension at an impressively nuanced level.

Let's look at the computational techniques behind Large Language Models' nuanced understanding of language. Recurrent neural networks (RNNs) are one of the first building blocks used, capable of processing sequences of data, such as sentences, and remembering past inputs. This memory characteristic lets them carry information about earlier parts of a sentence forward, which is essential for grasping context.

However, RNNs have limitations, which is where attention mechanisms come into play. These mechanisms enable a model to focus on different parts of the input text selectively, much like when you're reading and some words jump out at you, carrying more weight in a sentence's meaning.

The transformer model, a newer innovation, further refines this process. Unlike RNNs, transformers process entire text inputs at once, making connections between words no matter how far apart they are in the sentence. This ability is crucial for understanding the implied meaning, which is often not explicit in the words themselves but in how those words relate to each other across the text.

Training these models involves large datasets where sentences are marked with sentiments or context clues. For example, a sentence labeled sarcastic in the training data helps the model learn what linguistic patterns might indicate sarcasm, while a question tag helps it recognize inquiries, even if they don't end with a question mark.

Word embeddings and positional encodings are like the secret sauce in understanding nuanced language. Embeddings capture the essence of each word and its relationship to others, while positional encodings provide a sense of the word order, allowing LLMs to maintain the correct sequence of ideas. Together, they allow a model to detect sarcasm, distinguish rhetorical questions, and identify factual statements—key features for communicating efficiently.

Through these interwoven computational strategies, LLMs achieve a startlingly accurate simulation of human language understanding, discerning subtleties that make conversation natural and meaningful.

Picture Sherlock Holmes, with his keen eye for detail, piecing together the scattered puzzle of a baffling case to arrive at a solution that seems inevitable in hindsight. Large Language Models engage in a similar process, scrutinizing strings of text to generate coherent and contextually appropriate responses. They observe patterns and correlations invisible to the untrained eye—much like Holmes deduces facts from a seemingly insignificant speck of dirt.

Now, imagine being privy to the dynamic dialogue of a Jane Austen novel, where every line unveils character and advances the plot. LLMs emulate this by crafting text that isn't just a series of connected words but a pathway to deeper understanding and engagement, reflecting the characters' wit, values, and societal norms with each generated sentence.

Lastly, consider Tim Berners-Lee's creation of the World Wide Web, an intricate tapestry of information connected across the globe, much like the interconnected neural networks of an

LLM. These artificial networks weave vast amounts of information and language patterns into a coherent whole, producing text as accessible and expansive as the web itself.

In these scenarios, LLMs mirror the deduction, discourse, and connectivity that define some of the greatest leaps in storytelling and technology, showcasing their role not just as creators of text but as architects of understanding and human connection.

Here is the breakdown on how Large Language Models process and understand text:

- **Data Ingestion:**

    - Collection: Gathering vast arrays of text from diverse sources.

    - Cleaning: Removing irrelevant data to ensure quality.

- **Tokenization:**

    - Splitting: Breaking text into smaller, manageable pieces called tokens.

    - Normalizing: Standardizing these tokens to reduce complexity.

- **Word Embeddings:**

    - Encoding: Transforming tokens into numerical representations that capture meaning.

- Relationship Mapping: Embeddings also encode how words relate to one another.

## - **Neural Networks and Transformers:**

- Layers: Using multiple layers to process and understand the embeddings intricately.

- Contextual Parsing: Determining the relevance of each word in its given context through these layers.

## - **Attention Mechanisms:**

- Focusing: Honing in on specific parts of the text that are crucial for understanding the context.

- Weighing: Assigning importance to different tokens so the model knows what to pay attention to.

## - **Continuous Learning:**

- Feedback Loops: Incorporating feedback to refine and improve the model's accuracy.

- Updating: Adjusting the internal parameters to better predict and interpret new data.

Each part of this process builds upon the last, allowing LLMs to not just mimic human language but comprehend and generate text in a way that feels intuitive and sensible. As they go through these steps, the models become adept at detecting the subtleties of language, opening up possibilities for rich, natural interactions between humans and computers.

Imagine waking up to an assistant that not only reads your schedule out loud but also predicts your needs throughout the day, suggesting the best times for coffee breaks and meetings—all while ensuring you never miss your child's soccer game. This is just the tip of the iceberg when it comes to the potential impact of advancements in Large Language Models (LLMs). In the professional realm, these models could serve as ever-present aides, analyzing legal documents with precision or offering medical diagnoses by sifting through vast databases of research faster than any human could. On a grander scale, they might break down language barriers, facilitating real-time translation that connects cultures in a global conversation. The ripple effect of LLMs opens up pathways to communication that are currently mere concepts. Through this lens, the future of LLMs isn't just an academic discussion; it's a living, evolving narrative that weaves into the fabric of everyday life, transforming monologues into dialogues, and strangers into collaborators.

Let's look at the advanced features of Large Language Models and how they're being applied in various sectors. For personal daily assistance, LLMs use algorithms like recurrent neural networks (RNNs), which excel at understanding sequences and can predict one's schedule. They learn patterns in a person's habits and preferences over time, and use this data to forecast future needs.

In the realm of professional services such as law, natural language processing (NLP) techniques parse complex legal documents. These models are trained on specific legal terminology and can pinpoint relevant information, helping legal experts filter through extensive paperwork efficiently.

For medical diagnostics, deep learning models are invaluable.

They sift through immense databanks of medical images and literature much quicker than humanly possible. Using pattern recognition, they assist in diagnosing conditions by identifying anomalies that correlate with known symptoms of diseases.

Real-time translation is one of the most significant global advances provided by LLMs. It uses sequence-to-sequence models, which are adept at turning input from one language into an equivalent in another. These models consider the full context of phrases, not just word-for-word translations, enabling smooth and accurate communication across languages.

Exploring these computational powers offers a glimpse into how communication, both personal and professional, could be reshaped. By understanding how LLMs process and generate language, it's like peering under the hood of a car; you gain appreciation for the intricate engine that powers seamless journeys across the linguistic landscape.

Natural Language Understanding (NLU) is the driving force that enables artificial intelligence to converse, comprehend, and respond in a manner strikingly similar to humans. It is the foundation that allows machines to grasp not just words, but the intent and emotion behind them. With NLU, AI systems can interpret questions, provide answers, and even recognize when someone is joking. It's an ongoing dialogue between humans and AI, where understanding grows and evolves with every interaction. The future implications are profound: as NLU becomes more sophisticated, we're looking at a world where AI assists in everything from education to mental health, breaks down language barriers, and becomes a seamless part of daily life. In essence, NLU is not just about programming computers to understand language; it's about redefining the way we communicate and interact, ushering in an era of enriched human-AI relationships.

# ETHICS AND LLMS

We are now in the unfolding story of ethics in the world of Large Language Models, where advanced technology meets humanity's deepest values. As we journey through this chapter, you'll discover how navigating the ethical labyrinth is as critical as the technological marvels we create. These AI systems hold remarkable power, crafting language and engaging with users in ways once considered the stuff of science fiction. However, with great power comes great responsibility. This opening discussion lays the groundwork for understanding that ethics are not just a side note but integral to AI's future. Together, we'll explore the pillars of ethical AI, including fairness, accountability, privacy, and transparency, teasing apart complex concepts to reveal their significance in our lives and society. The goal here is not only to inform but also to spark a dialogue about the importance of steering AI development with a moral compass, empowering you to grasp the splendid potential of AI that respects and enhances our human experience.

In the realm of Artificial Intelligence, foundational ethics parallel the 'do no harm' principle esteemed in healthcare. Fairness, at its core, means AI systems should not create or perpetuate discrimination; decisions and processes should be equitable and unbiased. Accountability dictates that the creators and operators of AI systems are responsible for the outcomes, good or bad, ensuring they stand by their technology's actions. Transparency is about openness, allowing others to see and understand how AI models function and make decisions, promoting trust and understanding. Finally, privacy safeguards that the personal data AI systems learn from is protected and used ethically, respecting individual rights and freedoms. Each pillar acts as a compass, guiding the way AI develops and integrates into society, ensuring it serves to uplift rather than undermine, and operates under a code of honor that mirrors our collective conscience.

Let's look at the tangible steps to nurture ethics in Artificial Intelligence. To sow the seeds of fairness in AI programming, regular bias audits are essential. These are in-depth checks conducted on AI systems to ensure they treat all users equally. It's a bit like proofreading a document to catch errors that might give readers the wrong impression. AI needs similarly thorough checks to avoid unfair biases based on gender, race, or other personal attributes.

For accountability, which is making sure the AI can be held responsible for its actions, developers set up traceable decision-making processes. This means every decision an AI system makes can be followed back to the source, just like tracking a package to see every step of its journey. Establishing ethical review boards is also pivotal; these teams play the role of watchful guardians, scrutinizing AI behavior and ensuring it aligns with moral norms and regulations.

Transparency in AI is achieved through initiatives that aim to demystify how the AI reaches its conclusions. This is like a chef revealing the recipe to a signature dish—everything is laid out on the table for people to understand and trust what's gone into making it.

Lastly, privacy is shielded through techniques like secure data encryption, which scrambles data so that prying eyes can't read it. It's akin to sending a secret letter where the message is written in code, only understood by the sender and the intended recipient. Alongside, strict data usage regulations act as rules of confidentiality, ensuring personal information is respected and used correctly.

In focusing on these ethical pillars—fairness, accountability, transparency, and privacy—we furnish AI with a moral compass to navigate the complex digital world, charting a course that aligns with our highest human values.

Unchecked AI poses real risks, chief among them being the perpetuation of bias which can lead to discrimination. If a model is fed data that reflect historical prejudices, the AI may learn and magnify these biases, potentially affecting decisions in hiring, law enforcement, and lending. To prevent this, measures must be taken to identify and correct bias. This involves scrutinizing data sets for diversity and representativeness, as well as continually testing algorithms for fair outcomes. Transparency is also crucial so that the workings of the AI are not a black box but open to review and understanding by external auditors. In this way, by shining a light on the internal processes of AI and holding it to account, it is possible to steer clear of the pitfalls of discrimination and work towards AI that is just and equitable.

To ensure artificial intelligence serves everyone equally, building training datasets that mirror the rich tapestry of human diversity is paramount. This is done by gathering data from a wide array of sources, ensuring that the dataset encompasses the varied tapestry of age, ethnicity, gender, geography, and more to avoid skewing the AI's 'worldview'.

Once the data is collected, it must be scrutinized for any inherent biases—unintentional patterns that could lead the AI to make unfair decisions. Here, algorithms come into play, specifically designed to sift through data, almost like metal detectors scanning for unwanted biases beneath the surface. These algorithms are trained to highlight anomalies and patterns that may indicate prejudice, flagging them for review.

In the pursuit of transparency, audit trails become crucial.

Just as a breadcrumb trail can help you retrace your steps in the wilderness, audit trails in AI systems allow auditors to follow the decision-making path of an AI program, ensuring each step is justified and can be accounted for. Version control systems log changes in the AI's programming over time, akin to tracking edits in a document, ensuring that updates don't introduce new biases.

Opening the AI black box for all to see is where open-source reporting tools shine. These tools allow the code and algorithms of AI systems to be publicly available, similar to a chef sharing a recipe. By doing so, a community of savvy users and developers can review, suggest modifications, and collectively push for unbiased AI.

Walking through this process is a journey into the heart of AI fairness. It's systematic, requiring vigilance at every step - from ensuring diverse data at the onset to employing algorithms that detect bias, to embracing practices that support transparency and accountability. With these measures, AI can move towards becoming a just and equitable tool, bridging gaps rather than widening them.

Incorporating ethics into the development of Large Language Models is a bit like baking integrity into a cake from scratch. One starts at the beginning, with the design phase, where the intention for fairness sets the foundation. This means choosing training data that span a broad spectrum of human experience, ensuring no voice is left unheard. Next, the creation phase involves building models with mechanisms that can detect and sidestep bias, like a sieve that catches unwanted ingredients. After this, comes the refining process, where the model is tested and re-tested, identifying any ethical blind spots just as a taster tests each batch for quality. At every stage, a commitment to transparency keeps the process open to scrutiny, making sure everyone who uses the AI knows how and why it makes decisions. Finally, as the model goes into the world, ongoing feedback loops with users ensure the AI remains a tool for good, maintaining ethical standards long after it has left the drawing board. Through each methodical step, the LLM becomes a model of responsible AI, as reliable and trustworthy as a cherished family recipe.

Here is the breakdown on integrating ethics into Large Language Model (LLM) development cycles:

- **<u>Design Phase:</u>**

- Ethically Sound Training Data:

- Diversity: Ensure the data represents a multitude of demographics.

- Volume: Gather a large enough dataset to avoid overfitting to specific traits.

- Relevance: Include contextually appropriate data for the LLM's intended use.

- Guidelines:

- Consent: Use data that has been ethically sourced with consent.

- Legal Compliance: Adhere to data protection regulations, like GDPR.

111

- Documentation: Maintain comprehensive records of data sources and collection methods.

- **Creation Phase:**

- Techniques for Fairness:

- Bias Detection Algorithms: Implement algorithms that identify and mitigate bias.

- Regular Reassessment: Continuously test against new data to evaluate fairness.

- Objective Functions: Design models with inclusive success criteria that consider ethical implications.

- **Refining Phase:**

- Testing Layers:

- Internal Evaluation: Use a dedicated in-house team to test for biases.

- External Auditing: Engage third-party experts to provide unbiased assessments.

- Measures of Ethical Compliance:

- Performance Metrics: Establish quantifiable benchmarks for ethical behavior.

- Reporting Standards: Set up a clear framework for reporting findings and taking corrective actions.

- **Transparency:**

- Documenting AI Decision-Making:

- Open Models: Where possible, use open-source models to allow for public verification.

- Change Logs: Document all changes and updates made to algorithms and training data.

- Communication:

- Plain Language: Explain AI decisions and processes in language that users can readily understand.

- Accessibility: Make information about AI systems freely accessible to users and stakeholders.

- **Feedback Loop Mechanisms:**

- User Interaction Monitoring:

- Real-Time Tracking: Observe user interactions to help identify unexpected behaviors of the LLM.

- User Feedback Collection: Implement mechanisms for users to report issues or concerns.

- Performance Analysis:

- Continuous Improvement: Analyze feedback to refine and improve the LLM's ethical performance.

- Engagement Metrics: Monitor how changes to the system affect user satisfaction and trust.

Each step of this guide is framed with the intent to cultivate an LLM that is not only powerful in its language capabilities but also exhibits a respectful and responsible interaction with the world it serves.

Imagine stepping into a doctor's office where a virtual assistant, powered by an ethically developed Large Language Model, can understand and converse with patients from diverse backgrounds with subtlety and care. It's as if this assistant had spent a lifetime in every part of the world, learning how people speak, their cultural nuances, and medical histories. This AI ensures that each patient is heard and understood, providing customized care advice just like a compassionate nurse would do.

In the field of law, such language models would be akin to the scales of justice, meticulously balanced to sift through legal documents. They'd assist lawyers by summarizing extensive case files with efficiency, leaving no stone unturned – regardless of a client's socioeconomic status – ensuring fairness in preparation and study.

Now, picture a classroom where an AI, operating with the utmost ethical standards, offers a personalized learning experience. It would be like having a tutor for each student who adapts to their pace and style of learning, capable of answering questions in a multitude of languages and explaining complex concepts with ease.

In each scenario, the beauty and utility of ethical AI shine through as it enhances human efforts, making essential services more accessible, inclusive, and impartial – a true augmentation of the expert care, legal prudence, and educational nurture we value so dearly in society.

Here is the breakdown on the roles of ethically developed Large Language Models in key sectors:

- **Healthcare:**


   - Functionalities:


     - Multilingual patient intake to communicate with individuals in their preferred language.


     - Analyzing patient history and symptoms to assist with preliminary diagnosis.


     - Offering post-visit care instructions personalized to the patient's specific needs.

- Ethical Framework:

- Ensuring patient data privacy through secure processing and storage of personal health information.

- Data anonymization techniques to prevent identification of individual patients.

- Technologies:

- Natural language understanding for accurate interpretation of diverse medical terminologies and patient symptoms.

- Secure encryption algorithms to protect sensitive patient data.

- **Law:**

- Functionalities:

- Context-aware legal research that can comprehend complex legal jargon and provide summaries.

- Automated case law analysis to assist in legal strategy development.

- Ethical Framework:

- Unbiased information processing, avoiding discrimination based on any non-relevant case factors.

- Adhering to confidentiality and privilege regarding sensitive case material.

- Technologies:

- Machine learning algorithms trained on vast repositories of legal documents ensuring rich contextual awareness.

- Black box AI solutions to transparency, allowing for auditability of AI decision-making in legal assessments.

- **Education:**

- Functionalities:

- Adaptive learning modules that personalize educational content according to each student's learning style and pace.

- Language models that can evaluate and offer feedback on written assignments.

- Ethical Framework:

- Equitable access ensuring AI-driven educational tools are available to students of all backgrounds.

- Bias mitigation in grading and feedback to ensure fair treatment of all students.

- Technologies:

- AI-driven learning analytics to dynamically adapt instructional content.

- Feedback loops incorporating teacher and student input to continuously improve the learning experience.

Through careful design and application, LLMs enhance capabilities within these sectors, respecting the ethical imperatives of each field. These models don't just perform tasks; they do so while upholding the dignity of patients, the justice of law, and the inclusiveness of education, fulfilling the promise of technology as a force for good.

Ethics in AI is a subject as dynamic as the technology itself, shaping the way humans and machines interact. Each decision made today—be it on the data used to train an AI, the values embedded within it, or the consideration of its societal impact—sows seeds for future AI behavior. If ethical considerations are like a blueprint, then the machines we build now are the foundations of a house that future generations will live in. Design it with care, and it becomes a home that nurtures and protects its inhabitants. The principles that seem novel or peripheral today, such as fairness in algorithms or transparency in machine decision-making, will determine if that future house stands strong in the face of storms or crumbles when tested. By threading ethical deliberations into the fabric of AI development, we are essentially plotting a course for a journey alongside our mechanical counterparts, ensuring that as they learn and evolve, they do so with an ingrained understanding of what it means to serve humanity for the greater good.

Let's look at the ethical challenges in developing AI systems responsibly. Fairness in algorithms starts with the data—ensuring it doesn't reflect historical prejudices that could skew the AI's decisions. Think of this as creating a gourmet dish; one must start with quality ingredients that aren't tainted. AI developers use statistical methods to analyze data for biases and employ techniques like re-sampling or re-weighting to create a more balanced dataset.

Identifying biases is akin to a jeweler inspecting gems for flaws. Tools such as fairness metrics assess whether all groups are treated equitably by the algorithm. If disparities are found, they're corrected, much like a gardener prunes a tree to maintain its health and balance.

Transparency in AI is creating a clear window into how decisions are made. For instance, traceable logic paths in algorithms allow engineers and auditors to retrace the AI's reasoning, like navigating a well-mapped trail in the woods. Embracing open-source development is another way to promote transparency; it invites a community of developers to review and improve the code collectively, similar to a community garden where everyone contributes and has a stake in the harvest.

These foundational elements are essential in fostering trust between AI systems and the people who use them. Just as a house built on a strong foundation will stand firm, an AI built on the bedrock of ethical principles will gain and maintain the confidence of society. This steadfast commitment to ethics will pave the way for AI to be a trustworthy companion in our daily lives, enhancing our decisions, not dictating them.

In the landscape of AI, the role of ethics is not just supplemental; it's foundational. As we've seen, navigating the ethical terrain of Large Language Models is akin to embarking on a journey with a moral compass firmly in hand. From the data that breathes life into AI, to the algorithms that shape its decision-making, ethics ensures that our creations align with the core values of fairness, transparency, and respect for privacy. This attention to ethics does more than just build trust - it weaves the fabric of a future where AI acts in service of society, augmenting human capabilities without compromising human dignity. The critical discourse on ethics and LLMs brings clarity to the complexities of AI, ensuring anyone can understand and contribute to the conversation. It's through this shared understanding that AI can be guided to benefit all, not just today, but for generations to come.

# LLMS IN INDUSTRY AND RESEARCH

These LLMs are not just stepping stones but leaps forward, propelling sectors from healthcare to finance into a future where the written word is understood, generated, and analyzed by intelligent systems with an ease that was once the domain of humans alone. Picture them as master craftspeople, skilled in languages, capable of creating and understanding complex text, and imagine the potential this brings to every corner of the business and academic worlds. With each sentence they craft and interpret, these models are not only harnessing vast oceans of data but are also delicately entwining the threads of efficiency and productivity across fields, setting a new standard for innovation. This introduction is your gateway to understanding how LLMs work, why they matter, and what they herald for our collective journey alongside machines.

Large Language Models are revolutionizing the way businesses handle tasks that traditionally required a human touch. In customer service, LLMs serve as tireless assistants, available around the clock, answering queries with precision, and providing personalized help without the wait. Imagine a customer service agent who never needs a break and can speak to thousands of customers at once; that's the kind of efficiency LLMs bring to the table.

In finance, these models analyze vast amounts of market data to detect trends, generating reports that would take humans days in mere minutes, much like an expert analyst with a supercomputer for a brain. They sift through news articles, financial statements, and market signals to provide up-to-date insights, assisting financial institutions in making informed decisions.

Healthcare sees LLMs summarizing patient records and medical research swiftly, enabling healthcare providers to stay abreast of the latest studies and patient histories without drowning in paperwork. It's as if there's a knowledgeable colleague by their side, condensing hours of reading into digestible insights, ensuring patients receive the best care based on the latest information.

Through these examples, one can see how LLMs offer a helping hand, streamlining complex tasks and allowing professionals to focus on the human aspect of their jobs, elevating the standard of services across industries.

In customer service, Large Language Models operate by first being fed a stream of customer interactions – chat logs, emails, and voice recordings. Natural Language Processing (NLP) algorithms then help the LLM decipher language nuances. Picture NLP as a diligent language student, parsing through sentences, learning syntax, and recognizing sentiments. The training process involves feeding the LLM countless examples, a bit like a customer service rep going through an intensive training program with role-play scenarios.

Here's a simplified example resembling pseudo code that illustrates how an LLM might evaluate a customer query:

plaintext

Input: "I have been overcharged for my order."

Output: Analyze sentiment (negative), determine request

type (billing issue)

```
if sentiment == negative and request_type == billing_issue:

    response = fetch_help_article('billing_issues')

    take_action('issue_refund')

    return response + "Our apologies! We've issued a refund."
```

In the finance world, machine learning models analyze market trends by scanning figures and news. They might use a sequence of algorithms to filter noise, focus on patterns, and predict outcomes like a seasoned trader deciphering market signals amidst chaos.

With healthcare, LLMs sieve through patient records, extracting vital information akin to how a meticulous clerk might summarize extensive files. Trained with medical terminologies and case studies, they quickly highlight relevant patient information, much like expert diagnosticians who can join dots across symptoms and medical history.

Across these sectors, models are continuously refined as they interact with real-world data – like apprentices learning on the job, supported by sophisticated machine learning that adjusts to new patterns and outliers. It's a blend of structured learning from massive, curated datasets and adaptive learning from ongoing inputs and corrections.

Each step is a dance of intricate algorithms and vast data sources - a ballet where every move is precise and contributes to the performance's overall grace. This meticulous choreography ensures LLMs function synergistically within the frameworks of industries they serve, providing not just answers but insights precisely tuned to the needs of the querying human.

Researchers today are standing on the shoulders of AI giants. Large Language Models assist them by acting like high-powered microscopes that can zoom in on relevant literature from a mountain of data. In recent studies, for instance, LLMs have helped linguists decode complex language patterns by analyzing diverse linguistic data at scale. They parse through pages after pages, identifying correlations that might take human researchers years to notice. It's as if a team of tireless assistants read through every paper ever published, highlighting important passages and summarizing findings on command. Just as a skilled chef might combine ingredients in new and surprising ways, LLMs can combine pieces of knowledge to whip up fresh ideas, uncover patterns, and even suggest new areas for exploration. This is the silent, powerful engine of innovation in modern research, turning the vast ocean of information into accessible islands of knowledge.

Let's look at the sophisticated mechanics of Large Language Models in academic research. At the heart of these LLMs are multi-layer neural networks. Think of them as intricate circuits in the brain, with layers upon layers working together to understand language. Each layer has a different task – perhaps one focuses on grammar, while another picks up on the tone.

Deep learning techniques, such as recurrent neural networks, enable these models to process vast amounts of text, learning from context as they go along. In the case of sequence-to-sequence models, they're like meticulous translators, taking a string of text in one form and transforming it into another, be it a summary, a translation, or even a brand new idea, all while maintaining the essence of the original content.

Training these LLMs is an iterative process, requiring extensive and diverse datasets. It is comparable to educating a student, beginning with the basics and progressively working towards advanced topics with continuous evaluation and feedback. These AI students, so to speak, not only memorize but also understand patterns and connections within the data, developing an ability to infer context and deduce relationships between concepts. For researchers, this means AI can swiftly sift through scholarly material, identifying links and generating hypotheses that may have otherwise been missed.

To ensure these outcomes are accurate, validation procedures are critical. These are like rigorous peer review processes that academic papers go through before publication. The AI's conclusions are tested, errors are rooted out, and adjustments are made until the AI's performance is robust and reliable. Through these meticulous processes, LLMs are transforming into indispensable partners in academic research, opening doors to new realms of exploration and discovery.

Imagine a writing assistant tool empowered by LLMs as a savvy companion, whispering suggestions as you write, just as a seasoned editor would look over your shoulder, guiding you with improvements - except this assistant never sleeps, responds in seconds, and has read more books than a library houses. For streamlining legal document analysis, picture LLMs as the ultimate paralegal, one that can scan through thousands of pages of case law, statutes, and legal briefs, pulling out relevant information with the precision of a master craftsman selecting the perfect tools for a job. These LLMs don't just process language; they understand context and nuance, applying this grasp to create and refine text or to present just the right information from a stack of documents dense enough to make even the most dedicated lawyer's eyes grow weary. It adds a layer of intelligence to the mix, much like having a knowledgeable guide helping navigate through a forest dense with information, indicating which paths to take and what to leave unnoticed.

Here is the breakdown on how Large Language Models (LLMs) operate as dynamic aids in tasks like writing assistance and legal document analysis:

- Dataset Curation:

- Gathering a wide range of text samples, from novels to legal judgments, creating a data pool as diverse as a well-stocked library.

- Annotating data with labels to help the LLMs learn from context; it's similar to footnotes in a textbook explaining key points.

- Cleaning and processing the data to remove inaccuracies, much like editing a rough draft before publication.

- Algorithmic Pattern Recognition:

- Identifying parts of speech and sentence structures to understand grammar.

- Recognizing phrases and their usual usages to comprehend idiomatic language.

- Associating words with similar meanings, akin to a thesaurus in action.

- Steps in Natural Language Processing:

  - Tokenization:

    - Splitting text into meaningful units (tokens) like words or phrases.

  - Parsing:

    - Analyzing the grammatical structure of a sentence.

  - Entity Recognition:

    - Identifying and classifying elements like names of people or organizations.

  - Sentiment Analysis:

    - Determining the writer's attitude (positive, negative, neutral) as if sensing mood in a conversation.

- From Input to Output in Writing Assistance:

- Input: A rough draft or a piece of text.

- LLM breaks down the text into data it can analyze (tokenization).

- It checks the text against learned patterns (parsing, entity recognition).

- Suggestions are generated based on this analysis, offering improvements from word choice to sentence structure -- a digital form of editorial feedback.

- Output: The improved, suggested version of the text.

- For Legal Document Analysis:

- Input: A legal document, such as a contract or case file.

- LLM performs deep analysis, fact-checking against known law and precedent.

- Key facts and points of interest are extracted, similar to a paralegal's summary notes.

- Output: A concise report highlighting the document's salient points, potential issues, and valuable insights for legal review.

Each part of this process demonstrates the thoroughness with which LLMs handle textual content. These models are not just scanning words but interpreting meaning and intent, providing tools for professionals to work more effectively and efficiently. They can sift through the metaphorical haystack of data to find the needle of insight, making them an indispensable resource in both creative and analytical capacities.

Think of data privacy in technology as the confidentiality in a whispered conversation between friends. It's the understanding that personal information shared over digital channels should be shielded with the same respect as a secret entrusted to a close confidant. Just as any slip or breach of trust in a friendship can lead to discomfort and distance, the careless handling of data can erode trust between users and technology firms.

Bias in algorithms, on the other hand, is similar to a faulty compass that always points slightly off north. Even if the error is small, over long journeys, it leads travelers further and further from their intended destination. In technology, bias can steer decision-making in ways that favor one group over another, resulting in unfair advantages or detriments that, over time, have wide-reaching and detrimental impacts on society.

Accountability in tech equates to owning up to one's actions, like a cook taking responsibility for the meal they've prepared, whether it be a success or a mishap. When software fails or algorithms cause harm, being accountable means technology creators must step forward to correct the issue, much like a chef would rectify a recipe gone wrong, ensuring that those who partake in the digital world can do so with the assurance that their welfare is of utmost priority.

Let's look at the intricate aspects of maintaining ethics in the realm of technology, where the stakes are as personal as they can get — protecting individual data, ensuring fairness, and being accountable.

In the sphere of data privacy, technology utilizes a series of advanced tools and strategies to guard personal information. Encryption protocols act like complex puzzles, one that takes a supercomputer to solve, transforming data into a form that only someone with the right 'key' can understand, ensuring that even if data travels across the vastness of the internet, it remains unintelligible to anyone who might intercept it. Access control mechanisms serve as vigilant gatekeepers, allowing only authorized individuals to view or modify sensitive information — similar to a bank's safety deposit box that only opens with the correct key and permission.

Turning to algorithmic bias, the technology relies on a toolbox of methods to prevent skewed decision-making. It starts with assembling diverse and representative datasets — consider this as drawing from a full palette of colors rather than just a few, which helps in training algorithms to not overlook or misrepresent segments of the population. Fairness metrics are like finely-tuned scales, continually weighing outcomes to ensure no group is unfairly disadvantaged, and adjustments are made whenever the balance tips.

When it comes to accountability, systems like audit trails and error reporting are in play. Imagine an audit trail as a meticulous journal, chronicling every step an algorithm takes, so if something goes awry, developers can pinpoint where it occurred and why, much like detectives tracing clues back to their source. Error reporting mechanisms are akin to feedback forms, inviting users to report when things don't seem right, empowering those who design and maintain technology to take corrective measures swiftly.

Each of these components serves a crucial role in upholding

the ethical standards we highly value, ensuring that as technology becomes increasingly woven into the fabric of daily life, it does so in a manner that is secure, equitable, and responsible.

As we look toward the future, the integration of Large Language Models (LLMs) into diverse sectors heralds both exciting prospects and formidable challenges. Imagine these advanced AIs as a group of whiz-kids, each with a specific expertise fitting into various industry landscapes. In healthcare, they could sift through medical data, pulling out insights as effortlessly as a seasoned physician flips through a patient's history. In the realm of law, they might analyze legal texts with the eye of an eagle, spotting critical details that might otherwise escape notice.

However, the road ahead isn't without its bumps. Training these LLMs requires vast datasets, and much like a gourmet meal that starts with the freshest ingredients, the quality of these datasets is crucial. There's the ongoing balancing act of harnessing their capabilities while preventing them from perpetuating biases—ensuring they function as fair and impartial tools. Moreover, as these systems become more integrated into critical decision-making processes, their mistakes could have higher stakes, necessitating robust protocols similar to having emergency procedures in a science lab.

Circling back to their potential, if navigated wisely, the advancements in LLMs could redefine efficiency and innovation across industries. Yet, this new era demands a cautious hand on the tiller, steering the ship of technological advancement with foresight and responsibility. The key will be in crafting synergy between human oversight and AI's computational prowess to meet the complex demands of modern society.

Diving deeper into the technical side of LLMs at work in industry sectors, let's start with the algorithms. Machine learning models like neural networks serve as the backbone of these systems. Picture each node in these networks as a tiny detective, piecing together clues to make sense of language. The detectives work in teams (layers of the network) to analyze different aspects of the data, such as sentence structure and word meaning.

The training of these models is akin to a rigorous apprenticeship. It's not just about the quantity of text they read; diversity and quality are key. Training sets are like the world's most eclectic book club, encompassing every genre and style to ensure the LLM doesn't just understand text from one narrow perspective but can handle a wide variety of texts, from medical jargon to legalese.

Bias detection and mitigation are the processes that help keep the AI fair and impartial. Think of bias as a set of scales that are off-kilter. Techniques like re-balancing the training data and testing the AI against fairness metrics are ways to gently nudge those scales back to true balance.

Accountability is maintained through systems that track the AI's decision-making process, leaving a breadcrumb trail. This audit trail is like a detailed recipe that allows others to follow how the AI reached its conclusions, step by step.

Now, here's a snippet of pseudo code demonstrating how an LLM might process a legal document:

```
document_text = "Get content of the legal document"

parsed_text = NLP_parse(document_text) # Breaking the document into parts

relevant_facts = extract_facts(parsed_text) # Detecting and extracting entities like dates, names

case_law = find_case_law(relevant_facts) # Searching a legal database for similar cases

summary = summarize_findings(relevant_facts, case_law) # Generating a summary of the document and related cases
```

In this scenario, the LLMs NLP_parse function analyzes the language, the extract_facts function pulls out important details, and the find_case_law function searches for related legal precedents. Finally, summarize_findings combines these elements into a report, much like a paralegal summarizing a case for an attorney.

Each technical nuance from training to output choreographs the LLMs' ability to process and understand complex documents, providing invaluable tools for professionals across various industries.

In the grand tapestry of today's technology, Large Language Models hold a particularly vibrant thread, weaving through sectors far and wide with the promise of transforming how we work and think. The crucial takeaway here is the significance of crafting these tools with a mindful approach, ensuring their capabilities are harnessed for the greater good, much like a master watchmaker delicately assembles a timepiece, aware that every gear must align for flawless function. As these LLMs permeate various aspects of life, from simplifying legal complexities to enhancing healthcare decisions, the emphasis on responsible development and deployment becomes paramount. It's about ensuring each step, from initial data collection to model training and final implementation, is conducted with ethical considerations at the forefront, safeguarding against unintended consequences. Only through meticulous attention to these details can we fully leverage the benefits of LLMs and secure a future where technology augments human potential in harmony with our core values and societal norms.

# THE FUTURE OF LARGE LANGUAGE MODELS

In the early days of their existence, Large Language Models (LLMs) stand at a crossroads similar to the one once faced by the internet: poised at the brink of becoming a fixture in daily life. These advanced AI systems, which started as fledgling experiments in understanding and generating human language, now show the promise of altering the fabric of society. Imagine a tool so embedded in our routine that it feels like second nature—a tool that helps write articles, generates ideas, and even converses with us in natural language. Today's advances suggest a future where LLMs will be as commonplace as scrolling through a webpage, shaping interactions and opening new frontiers in virtually every field imaginable. While the path ahead is laced with unknowns, the potential of LLMs to enhance human potential underscores a thrilling narrative of progress— the evolution of these tools is not just a tale of technological achievement, but a beacon for innovation.

As we peer into the next chapter of Large Language Models (LLMs), we're likely to witness leaps in their ability to grasp and produce human language. Think of these improvements as sharpening a camera's focus, where LLMs will not only snapshot what words mean but also capture the subtleties in every picture—colloquialisms, tones, and even humor. With this enhanced clarity, these models stand to revolutionize countless industries. In healthcare, more intuitive LLMs could interpret patient queries and medical literature, providing diagnoses and health advice that speak directly to personal concerns. In finance, imagine them sifting through economic reports and global news to give advice that once required hours of a professional's time. And in education, LLMs could become personalized tutors, adapting to each student's learning style with content tailored to each individual's understanding. These advancements are like adding a skilled new member to each work team, one who can process and interact with information at an unprecedented pace, augmenting human expertise and creating new opportunities for growth across every sector.

Let's look at the forthcoming advancements in Large Language Models and their far-reaching repercussions on communication as we know it. Future LLMs might employ evolved neural network architectures that work much like a brain with an increased number of neural pathways, each fine-tuned to process specific nuances in language. Such sophisticated systems could entail Transformer models, known for their aptitude in handling sequences, which might allow an LLM to follow a conversation with the nuance of a keen human listener.

Advanced LLMs might also apply multimodal data processing to interpret not just text but images and sounds, grasping context from a patient's verbal description as well as their medical images. Imagine an LLM that can understand a phrase's meaning in the context of a relevant x-ray – a potential game-changer in diagnostics.

Training these systems could leverage enhanced machine learning frameworks like TensorFlow or PyTorch, incorporating complex algorithms that allow the model to learn dialects and idiomatic expressions by recognizing patterns within massive, linguistically diverse datasets. For instance, programming methodologies might include unsupervised learning, where the LLM discerns language patterns without direct annotation, paralleling a child's natural language acquisition.

In financial reporting, such enhanced LLMs could quickly analyze market trends from news and reports across the globe, spotting subtle economic shifts and sentiment much as expert analysts do, but at an unmatched speed and scale. In education, adaptive learning powered by these intelligent models could offer personalized instruction, akin to a tutor who understands a student's strengths and learning style and adjusts lessons accordingly.

In essence, these enhancements promise LLMs that not only understand and generate language as we do but can also interpret and act on multifaceted human expressions, bringing a new dimension to AI interactions across sectors. Such progress urges us to grasp both the immediate benefits and the more extensive implications of artificial minds fluent in the depth and breadth of human language.

Grasping the ethical considerations of deploying Large Language Models across varied sectors is a bit like understanding the rules of the road that keep traffic moving safely. Just as drivers must balance the freedom to explore new routes with the responsibility of following signs and signals, innovators must navigate the advancement of LLMs with a keen sense of ethical guardrails. This assures that these powerful tools enrich society without veering off into unforeseen consequences. Much like how genetic engineering is subjected to rigorous scrutiny to prevent unintended effects on ecosystems, each step in the creation and implementation of LLMs must be examined for potential bias, privacy breaches, and misuse. It's like a chef tasting a dish at different stages of cooking; continuous evaluation is essential for a palatable outcome. Balancing this exploration with caution ensures that LLMs serve the interests of all, functioning as both a powerful engine of progress and a precision tool honed with ethical craftsmanship.

Here is the breakdown on the ethical considerations when

deploying Large Language Models (LLMs):

- **Data Privacy:**

- **Consent:**

- Obtaining explicit permission from individuals before using their data for training models.

- Ensuring that data usage complies with privacy laws like GDPR or CCPA.

- **Anonymization:**

- Removing personal identifiers from datasets to protect individual identities.

- Employing techniques like differential privacy to further obscure data.

- **Transparency in Algorithmic Decision-Making:**

- **Explainability:**

- Designing models that can provide understandable reasons for their outputs.

- Tools and interfaces that allow users to query and understand AI decisions.

- **Documentation:**

- Maintaining clear records of data sources, model versions, and training processes.

- Creating comprehensive reports explaining the model's design and operation guidelines.

- **Avoiding Bias:**

- **Inclusive Training Sets:**

- Curating datasets that represent a wide spectrum of languages, dialects, and demographics.

- Regularly reviewing and updating data to reflect current societal norms.

- **Bias Detection and Mitigation:**

- Implementing routine audits of model outputs to identify potential biases.

- Algorithms that re-balance or augment data distributions

to reduce bias.

- **Ensuring Diversity in Training Sets:**

- **Sourcing:**

- Gathering data from diverse and inclusive sources.

- Collaborating with experts from various fields to ensure well-rounded training materials.

- **Conveying Model Decisions to Non-technical Stakeholders:**

- **Simplified Summaries:**

- Creating summaries of model activities that are non-technical but informative.

- **Tools for Interpretation:**

- Developing visualization tools to help stakeholders understand model behavior.

- **Monitoring and Mitigating Negative Impacts:**

- **Ongoing Surveillance:**

- Establishing systems for continuous monitoring of LLM impacts.

### - __Corrective Mechanisms:__

- Setting up protocols for prompt response and correction of any harmful model outputs.

Each element plays a crucial role in fostering a societally beneficial symbiosis between LLMs and their human users. By focusing on these ethical considerations at every stage of development and deployment, from data compilation to everyday application, technologists can cultivate trust and ensure that LLMs serve to augment human capabilities without infringing upon our rights or perpetuating societal inequities.

The research landscape for Large Language Models is as vast and varied as the ocean. One area that is rippling with potential is AI interpretability, where the goal is to make the thought process of these models as understandable as reading a book. Here, initiatives like the Explainable AI program by DARPA aim to create systems that lay bare the reasoning behind AI decisions. Imagine asking an LLM why it wrote a sentence a certain way and getting a response as clear as if you were asking a novelist about their character choices.

In the realm of general intelligence, the quest is to build LLMs that reach beyond specialized tasks, becoming as versatile and adaptable as humans in their cognitive abilities. Research efforts like DeepMind's quest for Artificial General Intelligence (AGI) seek to craft AI that can learn and master a variety of complex tasks, from composing music to solving environmental challenges.

As for enhancing language understanding, the field is

141

continuously advancing toward LLMs that can comprehend and respond to language with the nuance and depth of a seasoned linguist. Projects such as OpenAI's GPT series have shown progress in this domain, producing models that can simulate conversation, answer questions, and even generate creative fiction.

Each stride in these areas doesn't just push the boundaries of what machines can do; it opens up new territories for human cooperation with AI, fostering growth in every corner of society, from smarter healthcare to more responsive education systems. The impact of these research efforts promises a future where AI can serve as a bridge to overcoming the challenges humanity faces, making this journey not just one of technological innovation, but of collective advancement.

AI interpretability in Large Language Models usually follows several key steps to ensure the models' decision-making processes are as transparent and understandable as possible. To begin, developers might utilize decision tree algorithms, which mimic a flowchart-like structure to show exactly how an input leads to an output. Feature importance techniques are then employed to highlight what parts of the data had the most impact on the decision.

Taking a look at general intelligence, an LLM would need a broad set of traits to genuinely simulate human cognitive abilities. These traits include:

- Learning agility: The ability to learn new concepts and tasks quickly from limited data.

- Reasoning: Solving problems and making inferences based on incomplete information.

- Transfer learning: Applying knowledge from one domain to a new, different one.

Researchers might use benchmarks such as the Turing Test or Allen AI Science Challenge to measure progress, where an LLM must display human-like understanding and reasoning capabilities.

For language understanding, advancements have primarily come from neural networks, such as Transformers, that focus on the context of words within text rather than just the words alone. Training these involves large-scale datasets and techniques like reinforcement learning, where models learn through trial and error, refining how they construct sentences.

Here's a simplified pseudo code example of how an LLM processes and generates language:

plaintext

input_text = "What is AI interpretability?"

tokenized_input = tokenize(input_text) # Converts input text to a format the model can understand

contextual_analysis = analyze_context(tokenized_input) # Determines the context around the input

output = generate_response(contextual_analysis) # Produces a human-like response

print(output) # Could be something like "AI interpretability is making AI decisions clear to users."

Breaking down these complex systems unveils how methodical the advancement of LLMs is—from clear-cut algorithms that dictate AI transparency to nuanced language training methods that enable human-like conversation. It's a layered approach, ensuring that LLMs aren't just powerful computational entities, but are aligned with human intellect and societal norms.

Envision a day not too far in the future where Large Language Models serve as an invisible yet integral part of daily life. It's as if every person has a loyal, versatile assistant by their side, like the ever-present companions found in old tales of genies in lamps, but these are genies of words and wisdom. One wakes up to a gentle greeting from an LLM-powered device, offering a weather forecast tailor-made to one's preference, reminding about appointments, much like a personal secretary might.

Throughout the day, these LLMs act as professional consultants in various disguises: they help draft emails with the finesse of a seasoned copywriter, or they suggest recipes as a personal chef might, considering what's in the pantry. When confusion strikes over how to fix a leaky faucet, one doesn't fumble through manuals; instead, an LLM provides a step-by-step guide, showing the understanding of a skilled plumber.

As dusk falls, the LLM shifts roles again, this time to a mental health advisor. It listens and speaks in a soothing tone, offering comfort and resources, mirroring the empathy and aid that one would expect from a human counselor. It doesn't just recite preprogrammed platitudes but responds with thoughtful, personalized advice.

These LLMs, entwined with daily activities, are not just artificial intelligence; they are enablers of human intention, serving to amplify the capabilities and well-being of individuals. They navigate the complexities of human needs with the ease of a friend and the precision of a specialist, redefining the landscape of what technology can do for humanity.

Let's look at the sophisticated machinery humming under the hood of Large Language Models that allows them to act as nuanced personal assistants and empathic advisors. These models rely on a blend of complex algorithms, such as recurrent neural networks that loop information through their circuits, enabling them to remember and build upon previous interactions just as a good assistant would remember your preferences over time.

The interpretability of language—how these models understand the nuances of human communication—springs from things like attention mechanisms. Think of this as the model's way of focusing on specific words in a sentence, allowing it to grasp context and meaning like a sharp-minded consultant. For instance, identifying that 'running' a company has a different meaning than 'running' a marathon.

For LLMs to provide personalized responses, they undergo a rigorous training process. They learn from an extensive array of examples, a bit like an intern exposed to various workplace situations. Machine learning techniques such as unsupervised learning let the models detect patterns and preferences without direct guidance—similar to learning to cook by tasting rather than following a recipe.

The interface design, which governs how humans interact with these LLMs, must be as intuitive as the layout of a well-designed car dashboard, making sure that the essential features are accessible and that there's clear communication between the LLM and the user. User experience is paramount, ensuring smooth conversations free from the frustration of misunderstanding one's requests.

Feedback loops are akin to a seasoned performer tuning their instrument by ear after each show. These loops allow the model to improve and adapt by considering users' interactions and subsequent corrections or approvals, refining the LLM's performance progressively with each exchange.

Combined, these components equip LLMs to process and produce language that fits naturally into human interactions— whether it's scheduling meetings as a virtual secretary, sifting through advice as a financial consultant, or lending a digital shoulder as a mental wellness companion, they are poised to handle tasks with a blend of intelligence and understanding once thought to be the exclusive domain of humans.

In wrapping up, it's clear that Large Language Models are not just fleeting phenomena — they are catalysts for a new era, much like smartphones redefined accessibility and connectivity. Just as these pocket-sized devices turned sci-fi dreams into reality, LLMs are poised to usher in a wave of transformation, making robust human-AI collaboration a natural part of our lives. They stand to unlock human potential and streamline our day-to-day tasks with an intelligence that's designed to comprehend, engage, and evolve with us. From automating mundane chores to offering sophisticated companionship, LLMs carry the promise of a future where technology speaks our language and understands our needs, ensuring a synergy between human intentions and the limitless possibilities of artificial intelligence.

# CONCLUSION

As we turn the final pages of 'AI Foundations of Large Language Models', we take a moment to reflect on the journey traversed within these chapters. We have witnessed the remarkable evolution of Large Language Models, from rudimentary beginnings to sophisticated systems that understand and replicate the intricacies of human language.

Throughout this book, key themes have emerged: the power of data in teaching machines, the elegance of algorithms that decipher the chaos of human communication, and the promising horizon of AI's potential. We have learned that the essence of LLMs lies not in their code, but in their capability to bridge the gap between binary and the nuanced spectrums of human expression.

We grasp now the deep significance of LLMs, their development threading through the very fabric of modern AI. They have become not mere tools, but partners in dialog, creativity, and problem-solving—a testament to our ingenuity and a mirror reflecting our complex linguistic selves.

As we put this essential volume aside, let us carry forward the insights gleaned. May the knowledge serve as a bedrock for further exploration, fostering an ongoing conversation about the role of AI in shaping our future. In this dawn of linguistic machines, we find ourselves part of an unfolding narrative where our co-authored future with AI is beginning to be written, line by line, by the very Large Language Models we seek to understand.

# ABOUT THE AUTHOR

Jon Adams is a Prompt Engineer for Green Mountain Computing specializing and focusing on helping businesses to become more efficient within their own processes and pro-active automation.

Jon@GreenMountainComputing.com

Made in United States
Troutdale, OR
06/28/2024